This Is
Life Eternal

This Is
LIFE ETERNAL

BY
E. CLIFFORD NELSON

AUGSBURG PUBLISHING HOUSE·MINNEAPOLIS

THIS IS LIFE ETERNAL
Copyright 1949
Augsburg Publishing House

First Printing   January 1949
Second Printing   March 1949

Printed and Manufactured in the United States of America
by Augsburg Publishing House, Minneapolis, Minnesota
— 2166 —

To Lois

"Strength and dignity are her clothing;
  She openeth her mouth with wisdom;
  And the law of kindness is on her tongue.
  Her children rise up and call her blessed;
  The heart of her husband trusteth in her."

PROVERBS 31

Preface

The general theme of the following Lenten sermons is "The Moral Law and the Passion of Our Lord." Many writings have, in the past, been based on the Moral Law. Most Lenten books seek to unfold the riches in the Passion Story. This present effort brings the Moral Law and the Passion of Christ into juxtaposition. This, of course, is nothing unique. St. Paul, under the guidance of the Holy Spirit, did this and drew from it the basic tenets of evangelical religion. However, this study attempts to bring the Law and the Passion together as a subject for Lenten devotional reading and meditation.

The seminal idea for this Lenten study was born when, by a strange cooperation of circumstances, I happened to be reading a brilliant and persuasive presentation of the Ten Commandments, *Foundations for Reconstruction* by Elton Trueblood, at the same time as I was reading that Scotch work on the atonement, *The Death of Christ* by James Denney. The two streams of suggested thought merged in my mind and came out as a series of Lenten sermons on the Moral Law in relation to the suffering and death of the Savior.

The atonement becomes incredible and unreal if the consciousness of sin is extinguished or explained away. St. Paul's insight into the relation between law and sin is expressed in Romans 7:8, 9—"Apart from the law sin is dead . . . but when the commandment came, sin revived." Therefore, the further relationship between the death of Jesus and the law, through which the consciousness of sin comes, is a vitally significant one. This is not to say that the relation between God and man is only a disrupted legal and judicial relationship which is set right by the work of Christ. It is primarily a personal relationship. But to say that is not to say that it is a lawless relationship. It is both personal and moral. It is a personal relationship in which, ethically speaking, some things are forever obligatory, viz., love to God and neighbor. Moreover, some things are forever to be denied, such as hate, lust, selfishness. In other words, it is a personal relationship determined by law, and law which cannot deny itself. Without the understanding of that law, namely, the Moral Law, righteousness and sin, atonement and forgiveness, would all alike be words without meaning.

I wish to thank the Board of Publication of the Evangelical Lutheran Church which invited me to prepare these sermons. I am indebted especially to the following persons who read the manuscript critically: Prof. Leland B. Sateren, Dr. O. G. Malmin, the Rev. John Peterson, and Mr. J. K. Jensen. Finally, I wish to acknowledge with gratitude the encouragement which my parents, Mr. and Mrs. Martin Nelson, have given to me in my ministry and which, both directly and indirectly, has made easier the task of preparing these sermons.

E. C. NELSON

Acknowledgments

The following publishers and journals have graciously given permission to use copyrighted material and other quotations from their publications:

Abingdon-Cokesbury Press: George A. Buttrick, *Christ and Man's Dilemma;* William C. Skeath, *Thou Preparest a Table*

The Christian Century: March 29, 1944, and March 19, 1947

Doubleday and Company: Rudyard Kipling, *Mandalay*

Harper and Brothers: Elton Trueblood, *Foundations for Reconstruction.*

John Knox Press: Holmes Rolston, *Stewardship in the New Testament Church*

The Macmillan Company: Athanasius, *The Incarnation of the Word of God;* C. S. Lewis, *The Case for Christianity*

Marshall, Morgan and Scott (London): Samuel Zwemer, *The Glory of the Cross*

The Muhlenberg Press: Heinrich Boehmer, *The Road to Reformation;* Committee on Stewardship, *Stewardship Sermon Outlines*

Fleming H. Revell Company: G. Campbell Morgan, *The Gospel According to John*

Time, Inc.: February 3, 1947

University of Texas Publications: L. M. Hollander, *Selections from the Writings of Kierkegaard*

The Wartburg Press: A. T. W. Steinhaeuser, *The Man of Sorrows*

Table of Contents

PART I

PART II

Introduction

THE MORAL LAW AND THE PASSION
OF OUR LORD

WE FOLLOW in a good tradition of the Church when we make the Ten Commandments the subject of close scrutiny during Lent. Dr. Heinrich Boehmer in his book, *The Road to Reformation,* notes the fact that in pre-Luther days as well as during the Reformation itself the Ten Commandments were much used "during Lent as a mirror for confession." I am convinced that we are in an even better tradition of the Church when we seek deliberately to relate the Moral Law to the Passion of our Lord and to show thereby that God's great justice is but a part of that which is greater, namely, His love.

Elton Trueblood says the theme of his book, *Foundations for Reconstruction,* is that "the reconstruction of our world is not primarily a problem in engineering and not primarily a problem in politics, important as both are, but that the underlying task is to recover the sense of moral order. Unless this is the foundation of the temple of men, they labor in vain that build it."[1]

---

[1] Trueblood, *Foundations for Reconstruction,* page 100

1

Even as this is true of society ("the temple of man"), so it is also true that the Moral Law and the Passion of Christ are basic to the building of the Temple of God, "the holy catholic Church, the communion of saints." Indeed, they labor in vain that build it who, reading that "the law is good" (I Tim. 1:8), do not also perceive *"what the law could not do, in that it was weak through the flesh."* The Passion of Christ is the record of God's act in sending "his own Son in the likeness of sinful flesh and for sin . . . that the ordinance of the law might be fulfilled in us who walk not after the flesh but after the Spirit" (Rom. 8:3, 4).

No doubt it was the spiritual understanding of this truth that prompted C. S. Lewis, the modern British apologist for the faith, to write the following: "Christianity tells people to repent and promises them forgiveness. It therefore has nothing (as far as I know) to say to people who don't know they've done anything to repent of and who don't feel that they need any forgiveness. It's after you've realized that there is a Moral Law, and a Power behind the law, and that you have broken that law and put yourself wrong with that Power—it's after all that that Christianity begins to talk. When you know you're sick, you'll listen to the doctor. When you have realized that our position is nearly desperate, you'll begin to understand what the Christians are talking about. They offer an explanation of how we got into our present state of both hating goodness and loving it. They offer an explanation of how God can be this impersonal mind at the back of the Moral Law and yet also a Per-

son. They tell you how the demands of this law, which
you and I can't meet, have been met on our behalf, how
God Himself becomes a man to save man from the dis-
approval of God."[1]

The purpose of this Lenten study, therefore, is to bring
into sharp focus God's holy Law and His holy Gospel.
We must see clearly the relation between Mt. Sinai and
Mt. Calvary. We must understand that a straight line
runs from the Mosaic tablets of stone engraved with the
finger of God to the wooden cross that carried the body
of the God-man, Jesus Christ.

To achieve this there are four things which I have
done. In the first place, each of the Ten Commandments has been considered in itself, that is, in its unmistakable and simple prohibition or admonition. The
plain "Thou shalt" or "Thou shalt not" has been
pointed out. In the second place, the underlying sense of
the commandment, sometimes called its "spiritual meaning," has been sought out. For example, I have pointed
out that the Fifth Commandment is not only a prohibition against murder but the Moral Law's demand that
we exercise reverence for human life. In the third place,
in order to provide the appropriate Lenten atmosphere,
each portion of the Decalogue has been illustrated by
some character or incident drawn from the Passion
Story. In the fourth place, I have shown that every man
is subject to the Moral Law and is personally responsible
for his transgressions of it. This, coupled with the fact
that the weakness of human nature makes man quite un-

[1]Lewis, *The Case for Christianity*, page 27. By permission of the
Macmillan Company, publishers

able to satisfy the profound requirements of the Law,
should bring into bold relief the Word, "the wages of sin
is death" (Rom. 6:23). *The reward of transgressing the
Law of God is always death—either our death or Christ's
death.* It is only in the light of this that we can understand the Passion of our Lord. Although I have not felt
bound to follow these four points slavishly in dealing
with each individual commandment, I have, nevertheless, been guided in the general treatment of the whole
subject by this outline.

When we read the Old Testament it is well that we
remember that not all the laws are binding upon us as
Christians. We will understand this when we remember
that some of the laws of the Old Testament were temporary and were completely discarded with the coming
of Christ. The laws which God gave to the Hebrew people were of a three-fold nature: (1) civil, (2) ceremonial, and (3) moral.

The civil laws were a body of legislation which governed the political and civic life of the Jews. God was
using the Hebrew nation to prepare the world for the
coming of Jesus. During this preparation Jehovah ruled
their very civic life. Politically, therefore, the nation was
a theocracy.

The ceremonial laws were a body of legislation governing the religious life of the Jews. The law concerning circumcision, the law concerning the eating of pork (or any
of the other dietary laws), the laws governing the priest-
hood and the Tabernacle worship—all of these were
ceremonial and had fulfilled their usefulness with the

coming of Christ. At His advent the ceremonial laws, which had been a shadow of the coming Christ, were laid aside, for of what value was a shadow when the Person who created the shadow was present?

The Moral Law, written in men's hearts and made concrete in the Ten Commandments, was not cast aside by Jesus. He said He came not to destroy this Law but to fulfill it. He came to interpret its real significance for us and to obey it perfectly by His sinless life of obedience and to suffer the wages of man's sin against the Moral Law. The only part of God's ancient legislation, therefore, that concerns us now is this third part, the Moral Law.

To understand the death of Christ it is essential to understand this Law of God. Lutheran catechetical instruction is insistent upon one important Scriptural teaching, namely, that since the Fall of man into sin no person has the power to obey the Moral Law so as to be sure in his own soul that he has done all that is necessary for his salvation. One explanation of *The Catechism* asks, What good, or what purpose, does the Law perform, if it is powerless to save us? Note well the threefold answer:

First, the Law of God has as its purpose to show us our sins. Paul says, "Through the law cometh the knowledge of sin" (Rom. 3:20). Its purpose is to dig underneath our surface exterior, to show us our true nature, and to make us conscious, as Sören Kierkegaard says, that in relation to God we are always in the wrong. No one can know this except as his conscience is made sensitive by the Moral Law.

In the second place, this knowledge should alarm us and cause us to seek Christ. "The law is become our tutor to bring us unto Christ, that we might be justified by faith" (Gal. 3:24). The "alarm" of the Law is "set to go off" as we move about in daily life. Walk past the street-car conductor without paying your fare and the alarm goes off inside you. Your heart and your nervous system throb with the vibrations of that tiny alarm. The scientific gadget, "the lie detector," is based on the knowledge that we have a conscience sensitized by the Moral Law. But the distressing truth is that we can throttle the alarm. As with the alarm clock that rouses us in the morning, it is possible for us to shut off the alarm of the Moral Law and go back to sleep. In fact, some people become so adept at this that they can shut off the alarm while asleep and later contend with a loud voice that it never went off. Even more pathetic is the escapist, who tries to run away from the sound of the alarm. Rudyard Kipling's poem, *Mandalay,* pictures the man who seeks escape from the Moral Law:

> "Ship me somewheres east of Suez,
>   Where the best is like the worst,
>   Where there aren't no Ten Commandments
>   An' a man can raise a thirst."[1]

No matter how far "east of Suez" one is "shipped," there is no escape from the Moral Law. Indeed, a man

---

[1]From: MANDALAY from Departmental Ditties and Ballads and Barrack-Room Ballads by Rudyard Kipling. Copyright 1892, 1893, 1899, 1927 by Rudyard Kipling. Reprinted by permission of Mrs. George Bambridge and Doubleday and Company, Inc.

can shut off the alarm, but there is no escape. When this
is realized, the second purpose of the Law becomes clear:
it is our "tutor that brings us unto Christ, that we
might be justified by faith."

*A third purpose of the Law, which through "the flesh"
is powerless to save, is to restrain the predatory passions
of unregenerate men and to mark the path which Christians should walk.*[1]

It is the Law, not the Gospel, which will bring moral
order among peoples and nations of diverse religions and
cultures. To talk about "Jesus at the peace conference,"
when most of the peace-makers have not the slightest conception of the Gospel of the forgiveness of sins, is an
idealistic fantasy. Nations, said Luther, "cannot be governed by the Gospel." It is the Law, as Trueblood has
correctly observed, which is the only foundation for reconstruction in the world of men. The ecumenical
Church, as custodian of both the Law and the Gospel,
has a unique and oft-neglected responsibility, namely,
to be a witness to the *primus usus* of the Law.[2] This is
the obligation of the *whole* Christian Church, one which
Lutherans may and should assume together with others
who confess Christ. If Lutherans may not unite with
non-Lutherans except on agreement in the doctrine of
the Gospel and the Sacraments,[3] they may, nevertheless, add their voice to the voices of other Christians in
smiting the consciences of rulers and others in positions

---

[1] In this section I have included what Lutheran theology calls the
primus usus and the *tertius usus* of the Law.
[2] Jacobs, H. E., *The Book of Concord*, page 508
[3] *The Augsburg Confession*, Article VII

of influence with the Law of God. Unless the Church exercises this stewardship in the spirit and the power of the ancient prophets, it may find itself removed from its stewardship by the Author of the Law.

Still another use of the Law is to mark the path which believers should walk. The Law is not worthless to men of the Kingdom of Christ. No person who has accepted Christ as his Savior can safely dismiss the Law from his life. The wise Christian looks into the Law to be reminded of the fruits that faith should bear, and the lessons he fearns from this "tutor" constantly drive him to seek the forgiveness and strengthening of the Gospel.

———————

There is one more observation which I feel constrained to make before leaving these generalizations concerning the theme, "The Moral Law and the Passion of Christ." I refer to the divine imperative which Jesus consciously heeded throughout His Passion. The Father had sent Him to work out actively man's redemption from the curse of the Law. This was the divine imperative, the heavenly "must," from which He never swerved. At an early age He declared, "I *must* be about my Father's business" (Luke 2:49). How frequently that divine "must" appeared in the later words of the Son of God! "I *must* preach the gospel of the kingdom" (Luke 4:43). "I *must* work the works of Him that sent me" (John 9: 4). "As Moses lifted up the serpent . . . even so *must* the Son of man be lifted up" (John 3:14). "Other sheep I have . . . them also I *must* bring" (John 10:16). "The Son of man *must* be delivered up into the hands of sinful men and be crucified, and the third day rise again" (Luke 24:7). The divine necessity of the Passion of Jesus was not a dreary incomprehensible "something" which untoward circumstances forced Him to undergo. It was His vocation. It was given to Him, so to speak, along with "the form of a servant." As He unfolded His Messiahship to His disciples, He showed them that it contained death. Unceasingly He spoke to them saying, "He must go to Jerusalem and suffer many things."

Thus Lent can take on new and vital significance for us. As we walk quietly with Jesus through these days that bring us to Easter, we will be permitted to see the power and the fury of the Law spending itself in the Passion of our Lord. The Cross, in the words of St. Athanasius, will become "that monument of victory,"[1] and the Open Tomb will become the pledge that seals upon our consciousness the word of Jesus, "This is Life Eternal."

---

[1] *The Incarnation of the Word of God,* page 48. By permission of the Macmillan Company, publishers

Ye Call Me Master and Lord

THE FIRST COMMANDMENT

"I am the Lord thy God: thou shalt have no other gods before Me."

"Let God be God!"
—PHILIP WATSON

Ye Call Me Master and Lord

"YE CALL ME MASTER AND LORD: AND YE
SAY WELL; FOR SO I AM."

John 13:13

SOMETIMES familiarity breeds dullness. Our very
acquaintance with the words of the Scriptures
may produce a state of mind which leaves us un-
moved by the revolutionary message that God conveys
to us through them. If by some power we could completely blot out from our minds all remembrances and
impressions that have had their source in the Scriptures
—so that we could approach the Word of God as having
never heard or seen it before, as having no pre-condition-
ing of the mind and spirit—we would be overwhelmed
by the grandeur and the sublime character of the Word
from God about Himself.

This thought is in my mind as we begin our study of
the Ten Commandments and not least of this, the first,
that speaks about the eternal Being who brooks no rivals.
Pick up the Catechism of your youth and turn to the page
that says, "Part I—The Ten Commandments—In the
plain form in which the head of the family should teach
them to his household." There you will meet the majestic beginning of the Moral Iaw: *I am the Lord thy
God. Thou shalt have no other gods before Me.*

I

"I AM THY GOD"

The first thing the Law says is, *"I Am Thy God!"* This is the significant beginning to the Law. When we have paused long enough to get the tremendous weight of those four words, we turn to the thirteenth chapter of John, a part of the Passion History of Christ. There we read of that incident when Jesus washed the feet of His disciples before that last Passover Meal, which by His Word became the Lord's Supper. As He knelt to wash the feet of the disciples, He said, "Ye call me Master and Lord: and ye say well; for so I am." I think it is permissible to paraphrase: "You call me Lord. But I wonder if you realize what you are saying. Indeed, what you say is right, I am God; but you forget why I am come to you. I, who am God, now wash your feet. It is a part of my Passion. I am God who stoops down to save men. Even as I have stooped down and washed your feet to make you clean in body, I, the Lord your God, must stoop down even farther. I must humble myself and become obedient unto death, even the death of the Cross, the wages of your sin. This I must do in order that you may be *wholly* clean, not only in body but also in soul. You call me Master and Lord and you say well, for so I am. But remember when you say those words that I am what you say. *I am God.*"

There are two portions of Scripture which should be read in conjunction with this foot-washing scene where Jesus reveals Himself as the Lord who stoops down to serve. The first is "The Commissioning of Moses" (Exodus 3:13-15). "And Moses said unto God, Behold, when I come unto the children of Israel, and shall say unto them, The God of your fathers hath sent me unto you; and they shall say to me, What is his name? What shall I say unto them? And God said unto Moses, *I AM THAT I AM:* and he said, Thus shalt thou say unto the children of Israel, *I AM* hath sent me unto you . . . This is my name for ever, and this is my memorial unto all generations."

The second is the New Testament counterpart in the eighth chapter of John. The record is of the altercation between Jesus and the Jews. With ribald mockery the Jews say, "Thou art not yet fifty years old, and hast thou seen Abraham?" In Jesus' answer we meet one of those words where familiarity may have dulled our perception. *"Verily, verily, I say unto you, Before Abraham was born, I am!"* Pay particular attention to the formula, "Verily, verily." This Jesus used invariably to arrest attention and to emphasize the importance of what He was about to assert. And it was important! Jesus identified Himself with Jehovah, whose name for ever is "I AM." "I am the Bread of Life." "I am the Light of the world." "I am the Way, the Truth, and the Life." But now— simply "I AM." "Before Abraham was born, I am." Note that He did not say, "I was." That would simply mark "priority of existence." But the "I AM" claims *the eternity* of existence. He is Jehovah, the eternal One.

These words of Jesus make of Him either the most impudent blasphemer that ever lived on this earth, or God incarnate, Immanuel. "I am the Lord thy God."

II

"NO OTHER GODS"

The second part of the Commandment is stressed more often than the first part in our teaching. Therefore it is more a part of our religious consciousness: *"Thou shalt have no other gods."* The average Sunday school child is quite aware that many "things" compete with God for priority in our lives. Ask the children in the Sunday school, "What are other gods?" Immediately the answer will come back, "Idols, money, power, pleasure." Of course, the answers are quite right. But at this moment I want you to follow me as we pursue the thought which we sought to develop under the first part of the Commandment. We saw how Jesus identified Himself as being one with the Person who spoke, *"I am the Lord thy God."* Now the full force of these words, *"no other gods!"* comes upon us. "Ye call *me* Master and Lord: and ye say well; for so I am." *No other gods before Jesus!*

The God who stooped to wash the feet of the disciples and the One who died a human death for sin and because of sin says, *"No other gods."* It is our God, Jesus, who claims us. It is He who makes the First Commandment throb with compelling power. It is He who makes us see "the necessity of intolerance"[1] in a world that right now is wallowing in a mire of tolerance. The sobering truth is that we are not going to help save the world from its sin, from racial prejudice, from social distress, and from personal animosities by being evangelists for a gospel which says, "We don't care what you believe." We

[1] Trueblood, *op. cit.*, page 22

are not going to make any advances in peace and brother-
hood by obscuring all differences between men in a foggy
and gay good will. The gospel of tolerance which says,
"It doesn't make any difference what you believe," is a
fundamental violation of the First Commandment. The
Kingdom of God comes not by supposing that one view
is as good as another, but by heeding the truth and then
pursuing it with an unyielding firmness tempered by the
spirit of Christ. That is why Jesus strips all the pretty
wrappings from this hazy, good-natured talk about tolerance. He makes us "lose our respect for the merely tol-
erant man."[1] He shows us that the tolerantly indifferent
man is essentially a stupid man.

The point is that Jesus is God, or He is not. If He is
God made man for our salvation, that is tremendous
news, good news, the gospel. And one who is convinced
of it becomes intolerant of anything else. He knows there
can be "no other gods before Him." And he *does* become
concerned about what other men believe, for apart from
Jesus all men must suffer the wages of sin. The Scotch
theologian James Denney states it thus:

"I cannot agree with those who disparage this (Gal.
1:4, 8) as the unhappy beginning of religious intolerance. Neither the Old Testament nor the New Testament has any conception of a religion without this intolerance. The First Commandment is, 'Thou shalt have
no other gods beside Me,' and that is the foundation of
true religion. As there is only one God, so there can be
only one Gospel. If God has really done something in

---

[1]*Ibid.*, page 27

Christ on which the salvation of the world depends, and if he has made it known, then it is a Christian duty to be intolerant of everything which ignores, denies, or explains it away. The man who perverts it is the worst enemy of God and man; and it is not bad temper nor narrowmindedness in St. Paul which explains this vehement language (Gal. 1:8); it is the jealousy of God which has kindled in a soul redeemed by the death of Christ a corresponding jealousy for the Savior . . . Intolerance like this is an essential element in the true religion . . . Intolerance in this sense has its counterpart in comprehension; it is when we have the only Gospel, and not till then, that we have the Gospel for all.'"[1]

Of course, if Jesus is not Immanuel, God with us, it is high time we found out about it. We should unmask this two-thousand-year-old masquerade and eliminate this nonsense. For the awful truth is that, if faith in Jesus Christ as Master and Lord, as God, is not a true belief, it is a monstrously evil and wicked belief. Then we might as well confess openly that we have secretly made little tin gods of ourselves, of our machinery, of our business, of the atom, of power, of money, of pleasure, of success. But if Jesus is God, then there can be no other gods before Him. Then machines must serve Him. Then business, the atom, money—all must bow before Him. We must crown Him Lord of all!

Is Jesus your God? If you trust Him as your Savior, as the One who has fulfilled the Law and died for your transgression of the Law, you will behold Him as God, saying with Thomas, *"My Lord and my God!"*

---

[1] James Denney, *The Death of Christ*, pages 110, 111

CHAPTER TWO

He Began to Curse and Swear

THE SECOND COMMANDMENT

"Thou shalt not take the Name of the Lord thy God
in vain: for the Lord will not hold him guiltless
that taketh His Name in vain."

*"He who with fervency and inwardness prays
to some false god is to be preferred to him
who worships the true God, but without the
passion of devotion."*

—KIERKEGAARD

He Began to Curse and Swear

"HE BEGAN TO CURSE AND TO SWEAR, SAY-
ING, I KNOW NOT THIS MAN OF WHOM YE
SPEAK."

Mark 14:71

IT IS significant that the First Commandment places
God first. Indeed, if He were second, He would no
longer be God. It is also significant that the Second
Commandment indicates the possibility that He who is
first may be something less than first in man's devotion
and loyalties. Therefore, the underlying sense of the
Second Commandment seems to be that those who practice a mild, comfortable Christianity without the passion
of devotion to the Name of God are in reality taking
God's Name in vain.

Perhaps we ought to pause a moment and think about
the Name of God. What is meant by that? Sverdrup's
explanation of Luther's Catechism has a two-fold answer to the question, "What is God's Name?" First, it
refers to the proper names by which He is called in the
Scriptures, and second, to His nature and attributes, and
all that by which He is especially known, such as His
Word, Sacraments, and works. This is a good answer
primarily for the reason that it calls attention to the

fact that the divine Name is not limited to such words
as "Lord," "God," etc. G. Campbell Morgan goes so far
as to say, in his comments on John 17:6, that God has
only one name according to the Biblical revelation. He
says that "God" is not a name; it is a designation. "Lord"
is not a name; it is a title. God has only one name "and
his name is Yahweh—Jehovah, as we render it. Jesus had
borne it, linked with the thought of salvation. Jesus was
the Greek for Jehoshua, Jehovah-salvation."[1] So the
Name of God is that which is linked with His saving acts,
His Word, Sacraments, and works. Thus when Jesus said
in the High Priestly Prayer, "I manifested Thy Name,"
He had manifested to men God's desire to save man
from sin and death.

There are at least two ways in which this Name of God
is taken in vain. The one is the blasphemy which is profanity; the other is the blasphemy which gives cold as-
sent but not the passion of devotion to the saving Name
of God.

Both of these blasphemies are illustrated in that portion of the Passion History from which our text is drawn.
It tells of Peter, the man who began to curse and swear,
the man who promised so faithfully to follow Christ
come what may, and yet whose devotion faltered. Let us
remind ourselves of the event against the background of
the Second Commandment. Mark gives us the most vivid
account of the fall of Peter. And no wonder! Mark, the
interpreter of Peter, recorded the story as told him by
Peter. This incident had been indelibly etched on Peter's

---

[1] Morgan, *The Gospel According to John*, page 272

mind, and therefore the account in the Gospel which bears Mark's name is so graphic.

After Jesus was led away for trial in the Jewish court and before the high priest, Peter followed at a distance and somehow got into the courtyard of the palace of the high priest. We learn that Peter was not alone. There were soldiers, officers, and court attendants. It was early morning. The roosters had not yet crowed to signify the coming of the dawn. Against the chill and darkness of the night's last hours, these people had built a fire and were warming themselves. Peter joined the group. One of the palace maids, noticing Peter's face lighted by the fire, came up and looked at him intently and said, "Aren't you one of the followers of Jesus?" And Peter answered, "You must have mistaken me for somebody else. I don't know what you are talking about."

As he moved out of the circle about the fire, he heard her tell the men that she was sure he was one of those who had been with Jesus. Peter, hearing this, turned around and vehemently denied what she said. By this time the men around the fire were interested. The very vigor with which Peter denied any knowledge of Jesus made them suspicious. They began to pay attention to him. They noticed his face; they looked at his fisherman's clothes; and above all, they detected his brogue. He didn't talk like a city man. He had a Galilean accent. And when they were convinced of this, they turned on him and accused him of being one of Jesus' men. This was all Peter could endure. He lost control of himself and exploded with profanity. Peter had lapsed into an old fisherman's habit. Momentarily he was the man he had been before he met Christ, and he says of himself through Mark, "He began to curse and swear."

We are told by Luke that just as this happened Jesus was led through the courtyard. And Peter, seeing Christ look at him, was smitten in his conscience and went out and wept bitterly. Was not this the full realization of what it meant to take the Name of God in vain: not only the cursing and swearing, but the consciousness of having given mere lip service to the Lord Jesus Christ? Be that as it may, the incident brings into sharp focus the two blasphemies of which men are guilty.

The first is the obvious one of cursing and swearing. It needs no further illustration. We meet it every day On the street, in the factory, in the office, at school—in the grades, in high school, in the university lecture halls— the Name of God is blasphemed by men and women alike. And it is done with a flourish that suggests much practice.

Quintus Quiz, writing in *The Christian Century,* told of two Englishmen, good friends, who were out for a walk. One was contemptuous of his friend's religion. As they walked along, he said, "If your Jesus should meet us here as we walk, I would spit in his face." Instead of getting angry and leaving his friend, the other said, "It would not be the first time."

No, indeed, it would not be the first time. Let a man remember that each time his tongue turns to profanity he is spitting into the face of his Savior.

The second abuse of the Name of God is less obvious,

but it is a blasphemy as iniquitous as profanity. When lips form the Name of the Lord with a religious sound without a corresponding consecration of the heart and substance to the service of that Name, the spirit of the Second Commandment has been violated. There are hundreds, yes, thousands of folks, who cross themselves in pious horror when they hear people curse and swear and who themselves would not be guilty of saying "Damn!" or "By God!" Many of these, however, are just as guilty of sinning against the Second Commandment as the most profane traffic cop at the rush hour in the loop. Their blasphemy lies in that they say they believe but do little or nothing about it. They use the Name of God piously but without a sense of awe in the presence of that Name which is forever. The greatest danger to the Church today is not from the men and women who curse and swear and spit in the face of Jesus. We *know* they are enemies of God. We entertain no uncertainties about them. On the other hand, there are those inside the Church who do not practice their faith, those whose Christianity is mild and comfortable. They are the church members who confess the Apostles' Creed without enthusiasm. These people take the Name of God in vain; and the commandment says, *"The Lord will not hold them guiltless."*

This analysis of the Second Commandment of the Moral Law helps us to understand the oft-repeated statements which remind us that guilt before God comes upon us more frequently from the sins of omission than from the sins of commission. The purpose of this law, as with all the others, is to convince men of the reality of guilt, that it is not a psychological maladjustment which can be corrected in the hands of a clever psychiatrist. Rather it is that condition from which, as we confess in the Preparatory Service for the Holy Communion, "We can in no wise set ourselves free."

In the Passion Story the record says that Peter, the man who began to curse and swear, looked up and saw Jesus. It was then that he was smitten with remorse. He was convicted and alarmed. Christ was to die for Peter, "the just for the unjust."

This He did for all men, "that He might bring us to God."

Sanctify Them

THE THIRD COMMANDMENT

"Remember the Sabbath day to keep it holy."

> "New graces ever gaining
>   From this our day of rest,
> We reach the rest remaining
>   To spirits of the blest.
> To Holy Ghost be praises;
>   To Father, and to Son;
> The Church her voice upraises
>   To Thee, blest Three in One."
> —C. WORDSWORTH

Sanctify Them

"SANCTIFY THEM IN THE TRUTH: THY
WORD IS TRUTH."

John 17:17

THE difficulty of preaching on the Third Commandment is the feeling of futility which follows
upon it. Those who most need to hear it are not
in church. Of course, this can be said of all preaching,
but the preacher is most sensitive to this when dealing
with the duty of hearing the Word.

The characteristic, present-day American is not abashed
by his failure to attend church each Sunday. In fact, he
is a bit inclined to exult in what he considers his enlightened emancipation from ceremony and religious discipline. The Sunday services of worship in the church
which he attended as a boy represent the bondage from
which he has set himself free. To be sure, he exhibits
condescension toward his neighbor who has not advanced
as far as he has and who shows his provinciality by still
going to church every Sunday, come rain or snow. But
Mr. Modern American certainly has no inclination to
imitate his provincial neighbor's whimsical conduct. He
feels no deep-seated need which calls him to Sunday by
Sunday worship of the living Christ. The crudest and

most unintelligent expression of this twentieth century emancipation from church attendance is spoken by Mr. Solid Citizen when he says, "I get closer to God on the golf course than I ever do in the church."[1]

Our study of the Moral Law brings us now to the Third Commandment, which we shall consider in the light of a portion of Christ's High Priestly Prayer recorded in the Passion Story, "Sanctify them in Thy truth: Thy Word is Truth."

It is well at this point to think once more of the significance of the Law of God. I reminded you earlier of the *civil or political law*, of the *ceremonial or religious law*, and finally of the *Moral Law*. The last is the only part of the ancient legislation which is binding upon Christians.

The first truth concerning the Third Commandment is that it *was* (I use the past tense advisedly) both a ceremonial law and a moral law. That is, it belonged to that body of God's legislation which governed the religious life of the Jews, the ceremonies of worship, etc.; and it also belonged to the Moral Law, that body of permanent law which was given not just to the Jews but to mankind unto the end of time. Although moral and permanent, it has no power to save or to give life. Its purpose is to lead men to Christ.

This two-fold nature of the Third Commandment is really a most interesting and fascinating subject for study. The Third Commandment, peculiarly, is the only one of the ten which was both ceremonial and

[1]Trueblood, *op. cit.*, page 41

moral. This is a truth which the Seventh Day Adventist and Seventh Day Baptist Churches have not yet understood.

The second observation pertaining to this command is that, since Christ's advent, it is not concerned with the observance of any special day. Before Christ God regulated the ceremonial, religious life by saying, *"Six days shalt thou labor, but the seventh day is a sabbath unto Jehovah thy God."* The Third Commandment was definite legislation regarding a specific day of the week. Insofar as it spoke about a certain day, it was part of God's ceremonial law.

But it was also a moral law, then as it is now. It was a moral law in that it was based upon man's unchanging, permanent need of God. It was man's need of coming regularly into the presence of God to hear His Word and to worship in the company of other believers, in addition to his physical requirements for bodily rest, that gave moral quality to the Third Commandment. God spoke through man's need.

With the death of Christ every vestige of the ceremonial law was gone forever! The law of circumcision, the laws of diet, the laws of sacrifices, and the law of the Sabbath were at an end. This prompted St. Paul to write, "Let no man judge you in meat or in drink or in respect of a feast day or a new moon or a sabbath day: which are a shadow of the things to come; but the body is Christ's" (Col. 3:16-17). Every vestige of the ceremonial law was laid aside with the death of Jesus. We are free from the Sabbath ceremonial. We may worship on any day we choose. The great body of Christians has chosen the first day of the week, Sunday, in honor of the resurrection of Christ, for common worship and bodily rest.

The morality of the Third Commandment persists and will persist till heaven and earth pass away. Jesus said, "The Sabbath is made for man, not man for the Sabbath." As long as man remains what he is, he needs to obey the Third Commandment. In this sense the Moral Law is harsh with the "enlightened" and "emancipated" American. This Third Commandment annihilates his pretty philosophy about God's being "more real" to him on the golf course or out fishing than in church.

The moral force of the Third Comandment is caught up in Luther's Small Catechism where he explains it in this way: "We should fear and love God so that we do not despise His Word, nor the preaching of the same, but gladly hear and learn it." We conclude from this that we have every right to despise preaching which is not a declaration and proclamation of the Word, but absolutely no right to despise that preaching which is of His Word.

When our Lord died upon the cross, after having obeyed perfectly the moral requirements of the Third Commandment as well as the other nine, He died innocently for all our transgressions of this Law. He died for our lack of interest in His Word. Indeed, for every one of our sins of despising His Word, the sins which are evident in persistent absence from the House of God and in fitful, legalistic church attendance, Christ suffered and died, not that we might continue to despise His Word, but that, beholding "the Lamb of God," we might repent, believe we are forgiven, and then *"gladly* hear and learn His Word." No man is able to continue gladly in His Word without the regular discipline of Sunday worship. Elton Trueblood, whose book I have echoed so frequently, admits that church attendance is "an external support"; and, theoretically, a man ought to be free from external supports in religion. However, in order to be independent of external support, a man must be a spiritual giant. "The vulgar truth," he says, "is that most people . . . are not spiritual giants." It is conceivable that a man may have a great experience of God "while getting out of the rough by the seventeenth hole on a beautiful Sunday morning, but such an experience is really not likely to occur."[1] Why? Because, except in the most extraordinary cases, God has always chosen to call men *by the Gospel.* He enlightens them with His gifts *through the Word and the Sacraments.* These are found in the Church.

I have discovered that one of the soul's requirements is to be reminded of the need for fellowship with God through His Word in the Church. I think I am safe in assuming that this need is not peculiar to me, but that it is the common experience of Christians. Moreover, I have found that one of the chief functions of the majestic movement of the week that begins with the ringing of church bells on Sunday morning is to provide me with that reminder. Let me illustrate:

---

[1]*Ibid.,* page 41

Perhaps I already know the comforting cadences of the Declaration of Grace in the liturgy, but I am wonderfully helped in hearing each Sunday these absolving words: *"Almighty God, our heavenly Father, hath had mercy upon us and hath given His only Son to die for us, and for His sake forgiveth us all our sin."* Or, I may have heard the Benediction a thousand times, but I am always a better man after having devoutly received the ancient blessing: *"The Lord bless thee, and keep thee. The Lord make His face shine upon thee, and be gracious unto thee. The Lord lift up His countenance upon thee and give thee peace!"* The morality of the Third Commandment is that it keeps me reminded of my need.

Finally, there is a truth about the Third Commandment that embraces all that I have thus far said. It is the Word of our dear Lord as He prayed for us on the night before He was crucified: *"Sanctify them through Thy truth: Thy Word is truth."* What does that mean? It means, "Make them holy and keep them holy through Thy truth: Give them through Thy Word the holiness of forgiven sin, and guard them now and always from the power of sin." It was Jesus, the High Priest, who prayed that prayer. In the Jewish religion the high priest would enter the Holy of Holies on the Day of Atonement and there pray for his people. Standing before the flaming altar of the Tabernacle, he would pray for the tribes of the children of Israel. As we read John 17 we are in the presence of the great High Priest, our Savior the Lord Jesus. The Day of Atonement is at hand. Jesus is ready to ascend the altar of sacrifice, Mt. Calvary.

As He is about to enter that most holy place, He offers His priestly prayer for His friends. He prays not only for those disciples who had been with Him and who are with Him, but He prays for us. "He prays for all those who through the ages shall believe on Him. His mind is exploring the centuries to come. His hand is graciously reaching down through the generations until it rests in blessing on our heads."[1] Thinking of us, He prays, "Sanctify them through Thy truth."

Jesus knew the task that lay before the Church. For that task men need adequate equipment. Christians can not go into the battle empty-handed. They can never hope to bring the Gospel to every creature unless strengthened "not by might nor by power," but by the Spirit. So He prayed, "Sanctify them." Think of the Passion in those words! Here is the earnestness of Jesus praying for us before He died.

And how was this to be? "Through Thy truth, Thy Word!" That is why the Sabbath was made for man: in order that man might be sanctified by the Word of truth. That is why Luther, in explaining the Third Commandment, lays emphasis, not on the day, but on the Word of God. Thus the moral and eternal meaning of the Third Commandment is made clear in the Passion of our Lord.

Tell me, friend, are you a "spiritual giant"? Do you feel strong enough to miss church next Sunday and the next Sunday and the next Sunday?

[1]Skeath, W. C., *Thou Preparest a Table,* page 117

Behold Thy Mother

THE FOURTH COMMANDMENT

"Honor thy father and mother, that thy days may be long in the land which the Lord thy God giveth thee."

"We should fear and love God so that we do not despise our parents and superiors, nor provoke them to anger, but honor, serve, obey, love, and esteem them."

—M. LUTHER

Behold Thy Mother

"THEN SAITH HE TO THE DISCIPLE, BE-
HOLD THY MOTHER! AND FROM THAT
HOUR THAT DISCIPLE TOOK HER UNTO HIS
OWN HOME."

John 19:27

THE incident out of the Passion History which I
have chosen to associate with the Fourth Commandment is that in which Jesus provides a home
for His mother, the Virgin Mary.

I do not think there is any scene in the whole Passion
Story which has such a human appeal as this one. Because it is so human and so touching, it strikes a re-
sponsive chord in our hearts. Christ has been crucified.
He has uttered a prayer of forgiveness for His persecutors
and has pronounced absolution over the penitent thief.
Now He turns to His mother and remembers her in love.
He who died without leaving money, house or property,
nevertheless provided a home for His mother by asking
John to care for her all her days. He said to Mary, "From
now on John is your son." To John He said, "She is
your mother."

This beautiful saying not only reveals another facet
of the love of Christ, but it also blesses the *sanctity of*

the home. Jesus had little to say about the affairs of public life, nor did He give a blueprint for dealing with the problems of social and economic reform, but in His dying hour He was concerned about one social institution —the home. That is also the burden of the Fourth Commandment.

As we consider the Fourth Commandment, we are introduced to the *Second Table of the Moral Law*. All but the first three commandments of the Decalogue deal with our relation to society and to our fellow men. Therefore, as we enter into the social implications of the Moral Law, I want you to think of the Fourth Commandment and the word of the dying Jesus as the Magna Carta of the Christian home. Some of us are in a position to see the Fourth Commandment from two points of view. One view is that of a son or daughter whose parents are still living. The other is that of a parent who senses the responsibility of the home he builds.

Let us look briefly at the first of these, that is, what the commandment should mean to a son or daughter. This, of course, is its most apparent meaning and its usual interpretation. The word that meets us immediately is the command, *"Honor!"* There it stands like a sentinel on guard duty at the entrance to the Fourth Commandment. You cannot get into the Fourth Commandment except through the word, *"Honor!"* When we considered the preceding command, I thought of the word *"Remember,"* and how it stands at the beginning of the Third Commandment. We are commanded to remember! It is as if we are prone to forget the significance of the Lord's Day. Now we are confronted with the word, "*Honor.*" It, too, stands at the beginning, as if we are prone not to honor our parents.

One of the most frequently recurring experiences in family life is the cold ingratitude of thankless and thoughtless children. How many a father has suffered in dry-eyed pain to see the dishonor of a son! How many bitter tears mothers have shed over empty-headed and selfish daughters. Because this is one of the tragic *human* experiences, it finds a prominent place in the great literature of the world. William Shakespeare tells us of King Lear who is driven to despair by the ingratitude of his children. We recall the deep tragedy in his cry, "O sharper than a serpent's tooth is a thankless child!"

But perhaps the most poignant picture of a child's dishonor and a father's grief is the story of King David and his rebellious son Absalom. Do you remember it—how the handsome Absalom became conceited and puffed-up over his popularity, and how he organized a plot and rebellion against his father? He even had an army to carry out his plans. At last David was forced to send out the royal army against his own son. When the army went off to battle, each division passed in review before King David. As the soldiers appeared before him, he halted each division and spoke a message to the divisional commander. This was it: *"Deal gently for my sake, with the young man, even with Absalom."*

All day the battle raged in the forests of Ephraim, and finally Absalom's rebels were torn to shreds by the professional soldiers of the king's army. Absalom fled on horseback through the woods. Then it was that his beautiful, long hair was caught in the branches. Suspended from a tree, he was an easy target for soldiers' spears and arrows. When they cut down the body, they flung it into a pit. As each soldier marched by he threw a stone upon it, until a great heap covered the mutilated remains of David's beloved son.

In the meantime, the king was impatiently awaiting the outcome of the battle. At last a watchman on the city wall spied an approaching runner. He was quickly brought before the king. The messenger cried: "Tidings, my lord the king. God hath avenged thee this day." Straightway came the question that burned in David's heart. "Is it well with the young man, Absalom?" Then the messenger had to tell him of his son's fate. The king, bowed with grief, wrapped his cloak about him and stumbled up the stone stairs to his chamber. As he went, he could be heard crying to himself, "O my son Absalom! would God I had died for thee, O Absalom, my son, my son!"

Yes, the Fourth Commandment has been written not only on a tablet of stone; it has been written many times, again and again, in human experiences. All of them point to the sacred duty of sons and daughters to reverence those whom God has placed over them. The word "honor" stands at the entrance, and there is no way into the Fourth Commandment except through it. In the *Large Catechism* Luther emphasizes the word "honor" as being distinctive of the Fourth Commandment. He says: "God has exalted fatherhood and motherhood above all other relations under His scepter. This appears from the fact that He does not command merely to love parents but to honor them. As to our brothers, sisters and neighbors, God generally commands nothing higher than that we love them. He thus distinguishes father and mother above all other persons upon earth and places them next to Himself. It is a much greater thing to honor than to love. It includes not only love, but also obedience, humility and reverence, *as if we were pointed to some sovereignty hidden there.* . . . Thus the young must be taught to reverence their parents in God's stead, and to remember that even though they be lowly, poor, frail and peculiar, they are still father and mother, given by God. Their way of living and their failings cannot rob them of their honor. Therefore, we are not to regard the manner of their persons, but God's will that appointed and ordained them to be our parents."

There is another aspect to this portion of the Moral Law. Let us not forget that implied in this commandment is the injunction that parents must so teach and live the Christian life that their children may honor them. Think of what a grand thing it really is for a son or daughter to be able to say honestly, "Father never did anything that made us ashamed of him"; or "Mother's life was a constant testimony to Christ." What unspeakable pathos there must be in the heart of a child who sees his father a drunken sot or his mother a slovenly bar-fly!

In years past our present state governor, Luther W. Youngdahl, spoke before many church and civic audiences. How often he stressed the importance of this part of the Fourth Commandment, the duty of parents to live so that children have reason to honor them! There was a little poem he was fond of quoting. It went like this:

> A careful man I want to be,
> A little fellow follows me.
> I do not dare to go astray
> For fear he'll go that self-same way.
>
> I cannot once escape his eyes.
> Whate'er he sees me do, he tries.
> Like me, he says he's going to be,
> That little chap who follows me.
>
> He thinks that I am big and fine;
> Believes in every word of mine.
> The base in me he must not see,
> That little chap who follows me.
>
> I must remember as I go
> Through summer's suns and winter's snows
> I am building for the years to be
> That little chap who follows me.

Futile and empty are our goodness and affection without their testimony to Christ. We may give our young everything, but if we have not given them Christ, they are destitute. It is said to be a true story—at least, we know it is true to life—the story of the wealthy industrialist father who was deeply devoted to his son. He gave him all he needed and more—money, a Harvard education, a new home, a part in the business. When the young man was stricken with a fatal disease and lay dying, he looked at his father with an expression of utter despair. "Father," he said, "you gave me nearly everything. You have been good to me. But you never spoke to me about God. Now I am afraid."

Surely, your child is fortunate if he receives not only bread, education, clothes and culture, but also a living faith in Christ from your teaching and example. Then he will have the best possible reason for seeking to obey the Fourth Commandment, "Honor thy father and thy mother," and for knowing why Jesus, before He died for our transgressions, spoke to John out of His Passion, "Behold thy mother."

CHAPTER FIVE

He Hanged Himself

THE FIFTH COMMANDMENT
"Thou shalt not kill."

" . . . one hundred years from now . . .
'Europe . . . will have became a vast,
slightly radioactive wilderness, entirely
devoid of human life.' "
—N. H. PARTRIDGE
QUOTED IN *Time*, FEB. 3, 1947

He Hanged Himself

"THEN JUDAS, WHICH HAD BETRAYED HIM, WHEN
HE SAW THAT HE WAS CONDEMNED, REPENTED
HIMSELF, AND BROUGHT AGAIN THE THIRTY
PIECES OF SILVER TO THE CHIEF PRIESTS AND
ELDERS, SAYING, I HAVE SINNED, IN THAT I HAVE
BETRAYED INNOCENT BLOOD. AND THEY SAID,
WHAT IS THAT TO US? SEE THOU TO THAT. AND
HE CAST DOWN THE PIECES OF SILVER IN THE
TEMPLE, AND DEPARTED, AND WENT AND
HANGED HIMSELF."

Matthew 27:3-5

IN ONE of the city parks in Pittsburgh, there has
stood for many years a tree surrounded by a heavy
iron fence. On the fence is a metal plaque with this
inscription: "This tree was planted by General Ulysses
S. Grant." The purpose of the iron fence around the
tree is obvious. Because the tree had been planted by
a prominent man, there was a desire on the part of the
citizens of Pittsburgh to save the tree from the abuse
and vandalism of "the great American public."

In many respects the Moral Law is like an iron fence
which God has erected around certain sacred things in
life to protect them from sinful and vicious hands. We

49

have thought together about the iron fence which God has erected about the institution of the home, with its relation of parents and children. Presently we shall examine the guard which God has erected around sex, the relation between men and women, in marriage and out of it. At this moment, however, our concern is the Fifth Commandment, "Thou Shalt Not Kill." This is the iron fence which God has erected around human life.

That character out of the Passion Story who perhaps best illustrates this commandment is none other than Judas Iscariot. In a way it may seem strange to you that we have chosen him. Yet upon further thought you perhaps will see the reason. Here was a man who was guilty of violating many of the commandments:

The First—He did not fear, love, and trust Jesus above all things. He had other gods.

The Third—He despised the Word, which in the beginning was with God and was God, and which was now nigh unto him.

The Seventh, Ninth, and Tenth—He was greedy and covetous. He had an eye for himself, but not for others.

The Eighth—He pretended to be concerned about others, but he was not truthful. His lack of honor and his disloyalty to the truth culminated in his betrayal of the Lord.

The Fifth—Ultimately this man took the course of self-murder from which there was no turning back to Jesus in repentance. That disaster is always associated in our minds with the Fifth Commandment of the Moral Law.

Whenever I read the account of Judas' moral break-
down, I am impressed by one outstanding fact. That is
the fact that Jesus was so near to him at all times. The
availability of Jesus is a theme for all of us to ponder.
Even up to that last moment of bitter remorse and
despair, when Judas, convicted and accused, threw away
the thirty pieces of silver, even up to that moment there
was salvation for him, if he had turned to Jesus instead
of upon himself.

That is why, to me at least, Judas becomes such a vivid
illustration of the relation between the Moral Law and
the merits of Jesus Christ. In spite of all Judas' willful
transgressions of Moral Law, there was forgiveness even
for him in the sufferings and death of Jesus. *But there
was no forgiveness for Judas, for dead men cannot repent
of their transgressions of the Moral Law.* In this transgression the murdered and the murderer were the same
person.

One difficulty in preaching about the Fifth Commandment and in giving audience to this Word is the temptation to be superficial. Most folks who come to church are
not murderers. The preacher knows that and the man in
the pew knows that. Therefore, the whole consideration
is in danger of becoming impersonal, detached and aca-
demic—that is, of course, if we are superficial. If we have
not yielded to the temptation of superficiality, that
augurs well for our comprehension of the message of the
Fifth Commandment.

The sense of the Fifth Commandment is the sacredness of human life. It says to us that our bodies are God's temple. That is the only reason why human life has such a peculiar value. If a man is just a highly intelligent animal, or a rational piece of machinery soon to fall apart, then to talk about life as being sacred is absurd. The life of the body is precious either because it has already become or can become the earthly temple of the eternal God. And the Fifth Commandment is the iron fence God has erected around this temple in which He wishes to dwell. The Danish churchman, Grundtvig, has written a hymn, a stanza of which expresses the thought well:

> "Surely in temples made with hands
> God the most high is not dwelling.
> High above earth His temple stands,
> All earthly temples excelling.
> Yet He whom heavens cannot contain
> Chose to abide on earth with men—
> *Built in our bodies His temple.*"

I

DESTROYING THE TEMPLE

Let us look for a few moments at some of the ways this temple may be destroyed. Pastor A. N. Rogness reminds us in his book, *On the Way,* that a house can go to ruin either by what you do to it or by what you do not do to it. You can put dynamite in the basement and blow the house to bits, or you can neglect to repair it, to paint it and to care for it so that it gradually deteriorates.

It is so with God's temple, the human body, and the precious life which inhabits it. A man's life may be destroyed by what he does to it or by what he does not do to it. A man may destroy the temple by shooting himself, by drunkenness, or by gluttony. Or he can destroy himself by simply disregarding the elemental rules of sanitation and health. A man may kill his neighbor by thrusting a knife into his heart, by driving carelessly on the highway, or by refusing to share food with him when he is starving. In any case, he is destroying God's temple. The woman who jumps from the twentieth floor of a hotel or who prostitutes her body to evil men is destroying the temple where the eternal God yearns to dwell. Those who destroy unborn human life by devious and sinister methods of preventing birth must face the same accusation, *"Thou Shalt Not Kill"*—for this commandment applies both to the individual and to the race. In all these cases, man is breaking down the iron fence which God has erected around human life. He betrays the fact that he has lost the sense of the Fifth Commandment which is *reverence for life.*

Thus we begin to see the staggering implications of the Fifth Commandment in modern America. We are made aware of the truth that our Christian stewardship includes a deepening of our sense of the value and sacredness of human life, of the body as God's temple. That is why this command must embrace not only the negative, "Thou shalt not kill," but also the positive moral demand to love and befriend our neighbor.

II
CARING FOR THE TEMPLE

This is our stewardship. Elton Trueblood has said that one of our greatest needs today in the light of the Fifth Commandment is "the cultivation of an uneasy conscience."[1] By that he means that we have become hardened and calloused to death, to killings, to human suffering. We have read that Hitler killed five million Jews in gas chambers and concentration camps. We saw pictures of Buchenwald and Dachau. We read that 100,000 people were killed by one American bomb at Hiroshima. Overwhelmed by these horrors, we have been numbed by the magnitude of the moral disaster that has overcome the world. *The dreadful thing that is happening is the development of a good conscience apart from hearing the divine word of forgiveness.* When a good conscience comes to a man in any other way than through believing the Gospel, then "a good conscience is the invention of the devil" (Trueblood). The uneasy conscience, the sensitive, smarting, hurting conscience is the invention of God. It is God speaking to us through His Moral Law. There is no good conscience until first there is an uneasy conscience.

The thing that makes war so fearful is not that men, women and children die. But the diabolical thing is that war makes men forget that they are human beings, sacred human beings, individuals for whom Christ died. The Christian Church admits the necessity of participation in war under certain circumstances, but it teaches

[1] *Ibid.*, page 61

that war is still an evil, the lesser evil to be sure, but nevertheless evil. It tells Christians to view war with horror for it is spawned in the heart of the devil. The Church asks men to recognize it as a reminder of the devil's power over sinful men. It is out of the recent maelstrom that the Fifth Commandment speaks to us and demands of us what Dr. Albert Schweitzer calls "reverence for life." It is this great man, a versatile genius—musician, theologian, physician and missionary —who helps us in the midst of today's tangled ethics to look beneath the obvious meaning of "Thou shalt not kill" and see what God wants us to see, namely, that life is precious.

It is therefore a legitimate question: Where can men learn this "reverence for life"? How can men lose the hardness and callousness that permits them to read in the evening paper that millions of children are starving, and then to put down the paper and enjoy their dinner? How can men be made tender again? How can "the uneasy conscience" be developed? There is only one place and that is beneath the cross of Jesus. That is the only place where a man can learn again "reverence for life." There we see the Sinless One who obeyed the Law perfectly and yet died for the transgressions of the Law. There we see that the wages of sin is death and that the free gift of God is eternal life through Jesus Christ. That is what Judas missed. That is what anyone misses who scorns the place beneath the cross of Jesus!

CHAPTER SIX

Clean Every Whit

THE SIXTH COMMANDMENT

"Thou shalt not commit adultery."

'Wash me, Savior, or I die!"
—TOPLADY

Clean Every Whit

"PETER SAITH UNTO HIM, THOU SHALT NEVER WASH MY FEET. JESUS ANSWERED HIM, IF I WASH THEE NOT, THOU HAST NO PART WITH ME. SIMON PETER SAITH UNTO HIM, LORD, NOT MY FEET ONLY, BUT ALSO MY HANDS AND MY HEAD. JESUS SAITH TO HIM, HE THAT IS WASHED NEEDETH NOT SAVE TO WASH HIS FEET, BUT IS CLEAN EVERY WHIT: AND YE ARE CLEAN, BUT NOT ALL."

John 13:8-10

OUR study of the Moral Law and the Passion of Christ in relation to our salvation has brought us to the Sixth Commandment: "Thou shalt not commit adultery." Following the terminology suggested in the last chapter, this is "the iron fence" which God has erected around His gift of sex.

The public attitude toward the discussion of the Sixth Commandment has followed the path of the pendulum. At one end was a policy of "hush-hush," "see no evil, hear no evil, speak no evil." At the other end (where we are today) the evident objective is to "out-Freud" Freud himself. One wonders if the point of saturation has not already been reached. The prevailing unhealthy attitude towards sex makes a difficult subject doubly so. Consequently, when one speaks in public about the Sixth Commandment, he runs the risk of being considered as one who is seeking to draw attention to himself by saying something shocking or sensational.

At the outset let us attempt to remove one mistaken notion. This is it: To many people the term immorality usually means sexual immorality. The trouble is that most people get their theology by studying the newspapers rather than the Bible and the Catechism. The newspaper reporter writes that the "morals squad" of the police department brought a wagon load of characters before the judge, where they were arraigned on a so-called "morals charge." Thus there has been created in the minds of unthinking people the impression that morality or immorality is confined to the Sixth Commandment. Of course, this is manifestly false. We have been seeking to show during these Lenten days how a moral God and immoral men are reconciled through the Passion of Christ. In so doing we have learned that morality covers the whole relation of man to God and man to his fellowmen. The Sixth Commandment, instead of being the sum of morality, in reality is only a fragment of the total problem of morality.

We begin to realize this the more we penetrate the Moral Law of God. A man may be quite innocent of any sexual offense and yet be immoral. The person who stays away from church through contempt of the Word or the Sacraments is quite as immoral as the one who commits adultery. A non-lecherous man can still be thoroughly evil and detestable.

With that clear in our mind, we, nevertheless, must not minimize the immorality of which the Sixth Commandment speaks. In fact, one of the inescapable observations which we must make about society is that the sins against the Sixth Commandment down through history have been among the chief symptoms of a diseased and decaying civilization. Every nation, which has laid inordinate emphasis on sex by glorifying it as a license of men, rather than as a gift of God, has died.

America today leads the world in its rate of divorces. When we ponder this fact, it may not be so strange. The evidences of our American civilization—our business, our advertising, our pleasures, our literature—lead us to the conclusion that many of our normal pursuits seem to be dependent for their success upon the physical beauties of the semi-nude feminine body. The way to sell, the advertising genius says, is to give your product "sex appeal." This reached its complete absurdity at a recent builders' convention where an advertisement for cement mixers was enhanced by a bathing beauty seductively urging the buyers to consider the merits of this particular cement mixer. This would be laughable were it not symptomatic of a deep-seated, cancerous condition which is eating away at the vitality of American civilization. If our civilization ever loses respect for the Sixth Commandment (and it seems to be moving rapidly in that direction), just as surely as God is God and man is man our society will fall with a terrible crash, no matter how powerful we may be in an external way, no matter how many atomic bombs we have in the stock-pile. Unless we change our course, nothing will or can save us. And please, do not dismiss what I say as the rantings of a bigoted, uninformed preacher! No pastor can be alive in this year of our Lord and not have locked up in his heart tragic human experiences that reveal to him some of the depravities of which men and women who do not know Christ as their Savior are capable. Furthermore, there is no Christian physician or lawyer, or judge in the court of domestic relations, or social worker, who has not had similar, corroborating experiences. It is quite impossible to be alive today without being aware of the frightful ravages which are being wrought upon our society by *the devil, the world, and our own flesh* through violations of the Sixth Commandment.

Therefore, in the Moral Law God has erected "an iron fence" around this relation between the sexes—holy marriage. He has done so to protect us and our children from the corruptions of unchastity. Sex in itself is neither wrong nor impure. It is a gift of God, and what God gives us is always good. However, He seeks to protect what He has given us from adulteration, that is, from the invasion of impurity. Therefore, although marriages are not necessarily made in heaven, the institution of marriage is!

Perhaps now we are in a position to understand the mind of God in this part of the Moral Law. We have seen how in the Third Commandment God teaches reverence for His Word; in the Fourth, reverence for the home or family; in the Fifth, reverence for life; and now in the Sixth, reverence for the gift of sex and the propagation of the race. That is why unchastity among married or unmarried people is always a violation of the Sixth Commandment, for invariably the unchaste destroy reverence for God's gift.

That is why Jesus in speaking about marriage and divorce in Matthew 19:9 says: "And I say unto you, whosoever shall put away his wife, except for fornication, and shall marry another, committeth adultery; and he that marrieth her when she is put away committeth adultery." From this statement it is clear that Christ recognizes only one cause for divorce, and that is adultery. Although divorce itself is an evil to be abhorred by Christians, it is a step that may be taken without sin by the guiltless and faithful spouse. As with war, divorce under certain circumstances is the lesser evil, but, nevertheless, always evil.

Furthermore, speaking both to the married and the unmarried Jesus goes even deeper in interpreting the Sixth Commandment. In Matthew 5:27 He says: "Ye have heard that it was said, Thou shalt not commit adultery, but I say unto you, that everyone that looketh upon a woman to lust after her hath committed adultery already with her in his heart." Jesus traced all impurity to its source, namely, the heart, which without the grace of God is unclean from its birth.

George A. Buttrick suggests in his book, *Christ and Man's Dilemma,* the reverence which would follow were a picture of Calvary suddenly flashed on the screen of any movie theater in the midst of an incongruous setting.[1]

---

[1] Buttrick, *Christ and Man's Dilemma*, page 73

Perhaps he should have carried the thought a bit farther. Suppose that a picture of Calvary could be flashed on the wall during the stage performance at a burlesque theater. Can you imagine the scene? First, the sudden stunned silence as every eye is turned to the One on the Cross; the consternation and embarrassment in the bald-headed row up front; then the loud belligerent barking of the manager, demanding who is responsible for "this outrage"; and, finally, when the "disturber" has been evicted, here and there in the audience, young men and old men with downcast eyes and looks of shame quietly slipping out a side door without attracting attention, and hurrying home hating themselves.

Our Lord touched a sensitive nerve when He said, "He that looketh" with lust commits adultery. What about this? Must we be victims and slaves of our flesh? Can anything be done about this problem? Shall we perhaps do as the social worker did who had no Christian counsel to give to a wayward girl, other than the fact that society frowned on illicit romance? In a recent edition of *Our Sunday Visitor,* a Roman Catholic paper, there was an account of such a social worker's interview with a teen-age delinquent. The girl, in asking advice, complained that her parents had refused to allow her to spend weekends at an army camp with a boy friend. In attempting to dissuade her, the sociologist warned of the danger of venereal disease. The girl immediately countered that the boy did not have any. The next attempt was to suggest the shame of pre-marital pregnancy. The girl answered that the boy knew how to prevent this.

When the sociologist counselled that an accident might occur, the youngster concluded, "Well, I like kids anyway." The most pathetic display of ignorance and spiritual destitution, however, was made by the *counsellor* when she decided that the only argument left was "social convention"!

When King David had violated the Sixth Commandment, it was not the frowns of society that bothered him. His agonized and tortured soul turned to God and broke forth in the words, "Against *Thee, Thee only,* have I sinned!" That is the answer: the consciousness of sin against God. That is what makes the Passion of Christ so vivid. He was numbered among the transgressors, He was counted as an adulterer, so that we might no longer be under the curse of the Law but under the grace of God.

Jesus said, "Blessed are the pure in heart, for they shall see God." One wonders if that may not be the very reason why so few "see" God. Impurity has clouded their vision. David recognized this long ago when he prayed, "*Create* in me a clean heart." The pure heart is possible only through a creative act of God, such as brought forth the world and man in His image. Creation was through His Word. The pure heart is also created through the Word, the incarnate Word, who fulfilled the Moral Law and died innocently for the transgressions wrought by the impure in heart.

On the night in which Jesus was betrayed, knowing that He was sent from the Father and that He was returning to the Father, He took a towel and began to wash the disciples' feet. When He came to Peter, that impetuous disciple said, "Thou shalt never wash my feet." Jesus answered him, "If I wash thee not, *thou hast no part with me!*" Then Simon Peter exclaimed, "Lord, not my feet only, but also my hands and my head!" With that answer of Peter, our Lord spoke those grand words, "He that is washed is *clean every whit.*"

The death of Jesus to fulfill all righteousness and to suffer for sin is the only moral basis for our cleanness. It is what the hymn writer means in saying,

> "Let the water and the blood,
> From Thy riven side which flowed,
> Be of sin the double cure,
> Cleanse me from its guilt and power."

For this reason the same writer says, "Foul, I to the fountain fly, wash me, Savior, or I die." He that is not washed has no part in Christ.

Only as we believe that Jesus fulfilled the Law and forgives our sins are we "clean every whit." Only as we hide ourselves in the Rock of Ages are we free from the terror of having disobeyed the Moral Law. "For Christ is the end of the law to everyone who believeth," and He alone gives us the will and the power so to love and fear God that we may lead "a chaste and pure life in word and deed, and husband and wife love and honor each other."

CHAPTER SEVEN

For He Was a Thief

THE SEVENTH COMMANDMENT
"Thou shalt not steal."

"The acknowledgment of God's peculiar claim on a tenth of our income is not inconsistent with the acknowledgment of our responsibility to God for the use of all our income. . . . . It is fair to say that with most Christians the will to tithe has been born of the surrender of the soul to the infinite love of God which meets us in the death of Christ on the cross."

—H. ROLSTON

For He Was a Thief

"NOW THIS HE SAID, NOT BECAUSE HE
CARED FOR THE POOR; BUT BECAUSE HE
WAS A THIEF, AND HAVING THE BAG TOOK
AWAY WHAT WAS PUT THEREIN."

John 12:6

OUR Lenten study of the Moral Law in relation
to the Passion of Christ draws us once more to
the Book of Exodus, the twentieth chapter. This
time we center our interest in verse 15, commonly known
among us as the Seventh Commandment: "Thou shalt
not steal."

In the New Testament account of Christ's Passion we
frequently find reference made to Judas Iscariot, who in
so many ways illustrates graphically the transgressions of
the Moral Law. In connection with the Seventh Commandment we can hardly avoid this man. In fact, almost immediately we think of what St. John says, "Now
this he [Judas] said, not because he cared for the poor;
but because *he was a thief,* and having the bag took away
what was put therein."

Although we shall be thinking of Judas again, I believe we have reached that point where it is advisable to
pause a few moments to scrutinize this man more closely.

Why do we not name our sons Judas? It is a good name. It is as good as John, or James, or Paul, or David. In fact, in the Hebrew language the name "Judas" signifies "Praise." Furthermore, it is the name of a great hero in history, Judas Maccabaeus, one of the outstanding leaders of the Jewish nation. Yet we do not name our sons Judas. Of course, we all know the reason why. No matter how good a name may be, our likes and dislikes of it are determined by people who have borne that name. There is a perfectly good Scandinavian name, in fact, the name of one of the Scandinavian queens, which I could never give to a daughter of mine. You see, in my childhood that name always meant a certain unpleasant, toothless old lady who lived down the street from us. She hovered over my childhood like a bad dream. Memories of those days will ever prevent the use of that name in our family. It is for that same reason we do not name our sons Judas. It is a good name. It has a good meaning. It has a pleasant sound. Heroes have borne that name honorably. But the memories that cluster about one certain man make it impossible for us to use it today.

One of the keenest descriptions of Judas which I have read is by the Danish clergyman, Fibiger, who was pastor of the Elias Church in Copenhagen. He says that, in reality, at the time of the Lord's Supper when Judas slipped out into the dark shadows of the night, he was already dead. It was the beginning of eternal night! When he moved to betray Jesus, he was already a walking corpse, and Jesus had already delivered Judas' funeral sermon. It is recorded in Matthew 26:24, "The

Son of Man goeth even as it is written of Him: but woe unto that man through whom the Son of Man is betrayed! Good were it for that man if he had not been born."

Some people die long before they are buried. Judas was such a one. But his death was not sudden. Nevertheless, it came the way all death comes, through sin. To begin with, I am sure, Judas did not consider his stealing from the common treasury of the disciples as very serious. In fact, he perhaps did not even think of it as a violation of the Seventh Commandment. No doubt he was "just borrowing it." He may have had every good intention of paying it back. But when he saw that nobody seemed to miss what he was "borrowing," he became bolder and more regular in his pilfering from the purse. Finally, the Scripture says, "Then entered Satan into him."

This is the invariable course of unarrested and unforgiven sin. Though sin is never little to God, it usually seems insignificant to men. Judas did not start out to betray his Lord. The drunkard never starts out to be a drunkard. Perish the thought! His first step is the innocent social glass. He always boasts that he knows how to handle himself. He knows when to quit. The bank embezzler never starts out with any idea of huge sums. He pilfers, always planning to pay it back. Nor does the church member usually say, "Beginning next Sunday, I am going to stop going to church." Usually he misses one Sunday, then another. Quite soon it is easier to stay away than to attend. But he did not begin with the full-grown conviction that beginning on the sixteenth of March he was going to cease going to church altogether. No sin is a little thing, but it usually begins in a little, seemingly innocent way.

Dr. William Skeath, a Methodist pastor in Philadelphia, has written of this in his book, *Thou Preparest a Table:*

"Could our generation come to this sense of the reality . . . . , the potency of sin, it would take a long step towards morality. For all too many of us, sin is a thrill to be sought after, an experience to be desired for rounding out life—not an enemy to be dreaded. But sin is not a pet to be fondled. Dr. Woolston once brought before the children of his Philadelphia congregation a small lion cub, fondled it and petted it. Then by vivid words he made the children visualize the grown lion, sinister, dangerous, and deadly. It was a very effective method of impressing the children of his church with a sense of the dangerous nature of all human sin."[1]

After all there is no such thing as a little sin—or as our neighbors in the Roman Church say, "a venial sin." If a thing is sin, it separates from God. That is serious enough! The Bible wastes no effort in making fruitless distinctions between sin of one size and sin of another. Surely the cursing and depraved man is a sinner. No less is the cultured and well-educated person who places himself above the need of hearing the Gospel and looks down his aristocratic nose at the spiritually "bourgeois" practice of attending church. Both have "fallen short of

[1] Skeath, *Thou Preparest a Table,* page 52

the glory of God." The message of God's Word is that men are either sinners or righteous, and to be righteous is to be a forgiven sinner who is considered righteous by God because of his faith in Christ, the wholly righteous One.

The sin which is brought into sharp focus today is that against the Seventh Commandment, illustrated by the character and acts of Judas. His "little" sin of stealing was woven into the complete pattern of moral corruption that could only end in eternal night. He had not only been a thief, but he had wasted his life. Christ had given him a stewardship, but he had proved an unfaithful steward. How often Jesus had preached about the "deceitfulness of riches" in Judas' hearing, but that particular Word from God never seemed to penetrate his heart. He perhaps reasoned that Jesus was talking to the Pharisees or to the rich Jews, certainly not to a poor disciple like Judas.

Thus, you see that the real sense of the Seventh Commandment is the sense of stewardship. This commandment is infinitely broader in its scope than a mere prohibition against stealing. It is an admonition to Christian consecration of wealth and goods. This commandment relates money and property, earthly goods—ours and our neighbor's—to eternity. That explains how a man may be quite immaculate as far as the overt act of stealing is concerned and still be under the curse of the Seventh Commandment.

This, I am convinced, is the essence of a portion of the prophet Malachi's message, in the last book of the Old

Testament. Malachi records the words of Jehovah as a warning to His people: "I will be a swift witness against the sorcerers, and against the adulterers, and against the false swearers, and against those that oppress the hireling in his wages, the widow, and the fatherless." Notice how Jehovah emphasizes sins against the Moral Law: "sorcerers" violate the Second Comandment; "adulterers" the Sixth; "false swearers," the Eighth. He concludes with the Seventh: "Those who oppress the hireling in his wages, the widow, and the fatherless." This oppression of the hireling, the widow, and the fatherless is nothing short of stealing. But that is not all! He goes on as if to say, "You have been robbing your fellowmen, I know; but is it conceivable, is it thinkable, that you will rob *Me* too?" He admits that man plunders his fellowman, but it is almost incredible that man would turn upon his Maker and take what belongs to Him. So He asks, "Will a man rob God?" The people object. The accusation makes them bristle, and they ask heatedly, "Wherein have we robbed Thee?" They, like all men, thoroughly dislike being accused of stealing. But Jehovah answers, "In tithes and offerings! Ye are cursed with a curse . . . even this whole nation. Bring ye the whole tithe into the storehouse that there may be food in my house." God says to these people that they are robbing Him when they withhold the portion that belongs to Him.

To my knowledge, there is no *human* way of curbing this kind of stealing. If a man robs you of your car or burglarizes your home, he can be sent to jail. This threat of jail keeps some people from robbing their neighbors.

But we cannot send a man to jail for robbing God. We might hold over him the threat of eternal punishment, but that is hardly satisfactory either from the human or the divine point of view. God does not want slaves who fear Him, but friends who love Him. He seeks to create Christian stewards by pointing them to the Cross and trying to teach them to sing:

> "When I survey the wondrous cross
> On which the Prince of Glory died,
>
> . . . .
>
> Love so amazing, so divine,
> Demands my soul, my life, my all."

When an infant is born into the world, I am told that it is born with its little fists closed tightly. No doubt there is a physiological explanation for this tight-fistedness. I am interested, however, in the spiritual parable that it suggests. Human nature is born selfish. The modern psychologist may have another explanation for the child's possessive tenacity expressed so vividly and so piercingly when he screams, "Mine! Mine!" as he clings to his toys and playthings in the company of other children. The Scripture, however, says that this is sin from which we can in no wise set ourselves free, but for which we are, nevertheless, personally responsible.

Only the grace of God in Christ can open the tightly closed fist. And when Jesus is not given the opportunity to overcome that possessive tenacity, the child will go through life robbing God. He may be restrained from stealing by social customs and the frowns of society, or by the threat of jail and disgrace, but he cannot refrain from robbing God, who gave him life and breath, his reason and all his senses. Let Jesus come into his heart, let him be taught all things whatsoever He has commanded, then he will be aware that tithes and offerings are God's way of reminding us that all things belong to Him, and that the Seventh Commandment says, "Thou shalt not steal"—even from God!

CHAPTER EIGHT

What Is Truth?

THE EIGHTH COMMANDMENT

"Thou shalt not bear false witness against thy neighbor."

*"It is a curious paradox, but neverthe-
less true that we are more careful in
what we say about atoms than we are
in what we say about men."*

—TRUEBLOOD

What Is Truth?

"PILATE THEREFORE . . . . SAID UNTO HIM, ART
THOU THE KING OF THE JEWS? . . . . JESUS AN-
SWERED, MY KINGDOM IS NOT OF THIS WORLD
. . . . PILATE THEREFORE SAID UNTO HIM, ART
THOU A KING THEN? JESUS ANSWERED, THOU
SAYEST THAT I AM A KING. TO THIS END HAVE I
BEEN BORN, AND TO THIS END AM I COME INTO
THE WORLD, THAT I SHOULD BEAR WITNESS
UNTO THE TRUTH. EVERYONE THAT IS OF THE
TRUTH HEARETH MY VOICE. PILATE SAITH UNTO
HIM, WHAT IS TRUTH? AND WHEN HE HAD SAID
THIS, HE WENT OUT AGAIN UNTO THE JEWS AND
SAITH UNTO THEM, I FIND NO CRIME IN HIM."

John 18:33

I N THIS consideration of the Ten Commandments
and the Passion of Christ there have been four
things which we have sought to do. To heighten
our awareness of them, and for the sake of clarity, let us
recapitulate briefly.

(1) We have considered the commandment itself in
its unmistakable and simple prohibition or admonition
("Thou shalt not" or "Thou shalt").

(2) We have sought to look beneath the external pro-

79

hibition and see the underlying sense of the commandment, *e.g.*, the Fifth Commandment is not only a prohibition against killing; it commands reverence for life.

(3) We have illustrated the Moral Law by some character or incident in the Passion History of our Lord.

(4) We have endeavored to show that every man is
subject to the Moral Law, that he is personally responsible for his transgressions of it, and that through the
weakness of human nature he is quite unable to satisfy
the spiritual demands of the Law.

It is only in the light of this that we can understand
the Passion of Christ. The oft-repeated phrase, "He died
for our sin," is meaningless, a mere pious mouthing of
religious words by uninformed and spiritually uninitiat-
ed people, if the Moral Law is not seen in relation to
the death of Jesus. The Law demands perfect obedience
or death. No man can perfectly obey it. Therefore, by
right he ought to die. But the love of God has given
us Jesus. In Him we see the Law perfectly obeyed. In
His Passion and vicarious death we see the wages of our
sin innocently borne. In the Gospel we see His un-
matched merits of obedience and suffering graciously of-
fered to men under the tyrannical dominion of the Law.

This, in brief, is what we have sought to do in these
Lenten studies. Indeed, we have not always followed that
order nor have we always stressed each of these points,
nor shall we do so now in our scrutiny of the Eighth
Commandment.

Instead of dwelling on all the details, we hasten past
the obvious meaning of the commandment and cut

straight through to its underlying, spiritual significance. Let us call it "reverence for the truth." Notice I did not say "truth" but "the truth." There is a vast difference, a difference which I trust will become apparent as we proceed.

One of the most dramatic incidents of the Passion Story is the trial of Jesus before Pontius Pilate. It is dramatic, not in the action that takes place, but in the study of the characters who face each other and the conversation carried on between the two. That is tensely dramatic!

I presume all of us are familiar with the painting, "Christ before Pilate," by Munkacsy. Jesus appears worn and tragic as He stands with bound hands before Pilate's throne. Pilate is pictured in the painting as a typically aristocratic, patrician Roman. He has short-clipped black hair, beady eyes, and a thin-lipped, cynical mouth. He has a thoroughly forbidding, unscrupulous, selfish face.

Thus these two face each other. The picture is called "Christ before Pilate." In reality, however, the roles are reversed. The Prisoner becomes the Judge, and we should title it "Pilate before Jesus." For Pilate was confronted and judged by *the Truth*.

The trial has begun. Pilate is speaking. "Art *Thou* the king of the Jews?" There was contempt in his voice. This poor, tragic looking character certainly did not look like a king. The whole spectacle appealed to Pilate's sense of humor. It was ridiculous. However, he reasoned that he could afford to be indulgent and listen to the man. So, condescendingly he asked his question. But the answer was not what he expected. The Prisoner spoke not with excited, vehement affirmations of His royal claims. He merely answered Pilate's question by asking another question: "Sayest thou this thing of thyself, or did others tell it thee of Me?" The calm tone and the penetrating eyes of Jesus were disconcerting to the governor. He was not used to being questioned by his prisoners. He was caught off balance and burst into hot words: "Am I a Jew? Thine own nation and the chief priests have delivered thee unto me. What hast thou done?" By this time Pilate is quite finished with being amused by the situation. He is in a half-standing position, his hands on the arms of the chair, and his chin jutting forward. But his excitement is quite unnecessary. Christ's calm and quiet reply is disarming. Yes, He is a King. But His Kingdom is not like the many kingdoms of earth. If His Kingdom had belonged to this world, then His arrest would not have been such an easy and bloodless achievement.

Finally Pilate says, "Then you are a king after all?" The restrained but positive answer comes: "Certainly I am a King, a King who rules by the truth, and all who belong to the truth are my subjects." This is quite beyond the thick-skulled Pilate, and his lips form that famous but groping inquiry, "What is truth?" Not waiting for an answer, but turning his back on Him who is the Truth, Pilate shakes his head and speaks to the Jewish leaders saying that he can find no fault in Him.

I have said earlier that the underlying meaning and teaching of the eighth part of the Moral Law is "reverence for the truth," and I have also said that we shall be quite jealous about our use of the term, "the truth" instead of simply "truth."

Notice that in the conversation between Jesus and Pilate it is the latter who fumbles with the term "truth," but it is Jesus who says that He has come into the world to bear witness, not to "truth" but to "the truth," and who says that they who belong not simply to "truth" but to "the truth" are His subjects. Therefore, His Kingdom is the Kingdom of the Truth.

I have thought much and often about this recently. In this world of wonderful and brilliant people, how frequently men follow Pontius Pilate rather than Jesus. They grope after "truth" but are blind to "the truth." A man spends painstaking hours and years in a scientific laboratory surrounded by test tubes and atoms. He is searching for truth. It is an honest search by a sincere man. He is asking the question, "What is truth?" Every once in a while he gets a startling glimpse of truth, such as he has done recently in unlocking the secret of the atom.

But whereas truth has a thousand appearances, *the Truth has only one.* No matter how many glimpses of truth are found through the test tube or through the telescope, no matter how many aspects of truth are visible in Buddhism, Mohammedanism, Catholicism, Christian Science, or Communism (for there is truth in all), *the Truth* is but one, and it is made known only in a Person, Jesus Christ, who said, "I am the truth" (John 14). That is why our Lord said, "Ye shall know the truth and the truth shall make you free." Any interpretation of this last word apart from the person and work of Jesus tends to a philosophical, speculative, humanistic search for truth. When we seek truth apart from Jesus, instead of being made free by truth, we become prisoners of the means whereby we seek to know truth. Ours will be a bondage to test-tubes and telescopes, to laws of nature, to laws of mind, to laws of economics. Instead of freedom there is slavery. The purpose of Jesus Christ, the Truth, is to set men free from bondage!

In the final analysis, we understand that the Eighth Commandment is a law which is not merely a prohibition against false witness, but which is the positive admonition to have reverence for Jesus Christ who is the Truth.

Again, you see, the Moral Law leads us to Jesus Christ. The man who permits the Law to lead him to Christ, as the only righteous and atoning Savior, that man will enter upon an entirely new understanding of the Eighth Commandment, which says, "Thou shalt not bear false witness against thy neighbor."

He will see clearly that one of the most difficult organs in his body to control is his tongue. He will be ashamed of his tongue which so readily yields to gossip, to slander, to criticism, to half-truths, to white lies, and to faint praise of his neighbor. He will see himself as one of thousands of respectable people who would never dream of committing murder, adultery, or robbery, but who finds it easy and quite comfortable to sit in the parlor with friends and discuss an absent third party in a mildly derogatory manner. After all, the sin against the Eighth Commandment is such a pleasant one! It is only when one embarks on libel that he is in danger of prison. Most of the time the trespassing carries a sense of exhilarating excitement along with a sense of self-righteousness. For the man who talks destructively about his neighbor not only feels virtuous by comparison but places himself above the same criticism. Thus Luther showed great spiritual insight in saying, "Put the most charitable construction on all that he does."

The Eighth Commandment means reverence for the truth; the truth means Jesus Christ; and Jesus Christ in the heart means tongues under control, dedicated to bearing witness to the truth. Then like Jesus, the Truth incarnate, we must say, "To this end have I been born, and to this end am I come into the world, that I should bear witness unto the truth."

Why Was Not This Ointment Sold?

THE NINTH AND TENTH COMMANDMENTS

"Thou shalt not covet thy neighbor's house. Thou shalt
not covet thy neighbor's wife, nor his manservant,
nor his maidservant, nor his cattle, nor anything that is thy neighbor's."

"Covetousness is idolatry." —St. Paul

*"At first thought we do not always real-
ize the way in which covetousness becomes idolatry. . . . . The covetous man
can usually remain in good and regular
standing in the Church. But in the
long run the thing that rules our life
is the thing we worship regardless of
the professions we make to the contrary. . . . . From this point of view we
can see that covetousness may become
one of the most dangerous idolatries in
the life of the modern world."*
—H. Rolston

Why Was Not This Ointment Sold?

> "WHY WAS NOT THIS OINTMENT SOLD FOR
> THREE HUNDRED SHILLINGS, AND GIVEN TO
> THE POOR?"
>
> John 12:5

ONE of the rigid regulations of the Roman Church is the practice of private confession. The priests are expected to hear confessions from the people at specified times. In spite of the abuse of the confessional in some cases, this practice no doubt has a therapeutic value for the parishioners. At the same time it gives to the priest an indication of the moral tone of his parish. One of the better known missionary priests of the Roman Church was the Jesuit, Francis Xavier, who introduced Catholicism to India, Japan and China. He is reported to have made this statement which I quote as an introduction to our study of the Ninth and Tenth Commandments:

"I have had many people resort to me for confession. The confession of every sin that I have known or heard of, and sins so foul that I never dreamed of them, has been poured into my ear. *But no person has ever confessed to me the sin of covetousness.*"

I think that most non-Roman pastors can say the same thing. It is common for pastors to be confronted with the sins of blasphemy of the name of God, of dishonoring the Lord's Day, of family trouble, of drunkenness, of adultery, of theft—but like Francis Xavier, most Christian pastors can say, "I have never had a person come to me with a problem which he confesses is the sin of covetousness." Have you wondered about this? Certainly covetousness is a common sin. Dr. A. A. Zinck says deliberately, "There is no sin which more prominently and more destructively opposes the influence of the Gospel than the sin of covetousness. . . ." He continues: "Every pastor knows too well of members who are in the grip of covetousness. He has seen them regular in attendance at the services of the church, yet apparently experiencing little growth in the Christian graces. . . ."[1]

Now the question: How can we explain this strange enigma? We are faced with the obvious prevalence and universality of this sin against the Ninth and Tenth Commandments, and still it very seldom comes out into the open. What is the explanation?

I believe the answer lies in the *nature* of the sin of covetousness. This last part of God's Moral Law is the most difficult of all because it deals with the root and source of all sin. It is an "underground" sin, if we may call it that. Its presence is usually revealed through other sins. We tend to concentrate on these and to miss covetousness. It is most closely related to what the old theologians called "concupiscence," or "the capacity to sin."

[1] *Stewardship Sermon Outlines*, pages 75, 76

The word "covet" as used most frequently in the Bible means "evil desire" or simply "greed." That perhaps explains better than anything else the difficulty of this part of the Law dealing, as it does, with that illusive and most intangible thing which we call the will. Of course, that is what Jesus did with all transgression of the Moral Law, tracing it back to the will and to the thoughts of men. He made hate equivalent to murder, and the lustful look equivalent to adultery. But in the Law concerning covetousness we are ushered into the very center of a man's life even without the benefit of the teaching of Jesus.

I have wondered for some time why God placed covetousness at the end of the Moral Law. I think I understand now. Covetousness is seen most often in connection with money, and is, therefore, interpreted as greed for money. Perhaps we have failed to see that this sin is greater than any specific greed. As a matter of fact, there are covetous people who are not greedy for money. One man may have greed for praise, another for position or power, or for "good standing" in the eyes of his fellows. Consequently, his whole life may be dominated by covetousness, and yet be quite free from the financial concern which relates to covetousness. Thus it is a part of the wisdom of God that He places this commandment at the end of the Moral Law, so that we may recognize the underlying danger to all moral living. When we think of the different commandments—the Third: reverence for the Word, the Fifth: reverence for life, the Sixth: reverence for sex, the Seventh: reverence for stewardship—there is a sin, the sin of covetousness, that brings our Sunday worship, our home life, our stewardship into constant jeopardy. "The pervasive fact of human greed" (Trueblood) constantly endangers the whole moral structure of man. God has placed this law at the end as a forceful reminder of our inherent weakness. St. Paul recognized this quite clearly when he said, "Covetousness is idolatry." By that definition he tied the First Commandment to the Ninth and Tenth Commandments. He brought together "Thou shalt have no other gods" and "Thou shalt not covet," and the Moral Law became a complete circle.

That is the wisdom of God in reserving the commandment about covetousness for the last. It shows us that this sin in its essence is the same as the sin against the First Commandment, which is an absence of fear, love, and trust in God above all things. Covetousness, too, is the absence of fear, love and trust in God. Covetousness is idolatry.

Thus the Moral Law is an organic whole, a unit. Just as God is not divided, so the Law of God is not divided. It begins in God and it ends in Him who said, "I am the Alpha and the Omega, the beginning and the end."

I believe we are ready now to turn to the Passion Story for an incident that illustrates covetousness. We do not have to seek very far. The Holy Week record opens with an account of the evening before Palm Sunday, that is, the evening of the Sabbath Day. That opening account is where we pause. Jesus and His disciples are having supper in the village of Bethany at the home of Mary,

Martha and Lazarus. It was a home where Jesus was always welcome. And why should He not be welcome? There sat Lazarus, the resurrected one, the one who was dead but now was alive by the word of Jesus, a living testimony to the might and the goodness of the Son of God. Surely Jesus was always welcome at Bethany.

While they were eating, Mary did something strange. She brought a jar of perfumed, expensive oil, poured it over the feet of Jesus, and then kneeled to dry His feet with her hair. While she did that, the disciple John heard Judas mutter, "Why was not this ointment sold for three hundred shillings and given to the poor?" John, knowing what happened later, added these significant explanatory words, "Now this he said, not because he cared for the poor, but because he was a thief."

I am convinced that here we have a well-nigh perfect illustration of the total meaning of the word, "Thou shalt not covet." This command not only prohibits greed, but like all the others expects the practice of that which is the opposite. When we look for the opposite of greed or covetousness, we must find a loving, selfless heart. That is why this story of the anointing at Bethany is such a satisfying example of what I mean to convey through this study. Here we have a picture of Judas and Mary, the one wholly covetous, the other wholly loving.

In the character of Judas we have one more of these unpleasant, dark pictures of human sin. The thing that makes this so emphatic to us today is that Judas' words, "Why was not this ointment sold?" reveal a thoroughly evil heart, a covetous spirit, which really was the cause of all his other troubles—murder, theft, false witness, etc. It shows that the pervasive character of covetousness endangers the whole of life, and it proves that the Ninth and Tenth Commandments are placed at the end for a purpose: to emphasize the finality with which God judges human sin.

The counterpart of covetousness is found in the beautiful picture of Mary's loving act. In one completely selfless and devoted service she poured out that expensive perfume on the body of Jesus. I suppose that to the person who has never experienced the love of God this act of Mary seems overdone and a bit silly. It appears to have no other value than to satisfy the whims and the unstable nature of a purely sentimental woman.

But to Christ it was the expression of a good heart. In fact, He said, "She hath wrought a good work upon me." I want you to note that this is the only time in the Scriptures that Christ called anyone's work a good work. It was good because it came from a good heart. By nature Mary's heart was no better than Judas' heart. Both were born in iniquity and needed to be born again by the incorruptible seed, the Word of God. The one who was born again heard Jesus say that she had done a good work, a good work which had proceeded from a good heart. The other, who was not born again by the Word which was "nigh unto him," heard the Word say to him, "That which thou doest, do quickly!" Unmistakably the two-fold teaching of this command is made plain in this little story of the anointing at Bethany.

As I have studied the law about covetousness and have

been persuaded that no man is free of this deadly disease, I am more and more impressed by what St. Paul says about Jesus, *"He who knew no sin was made to be sin."* The utterly selfless and non-covetous One so completely identified Himself with covetous humanity that He became covetousness for us and suffered its guilt and punishment, eternal death. That eternity of death was compressed into one awful, shuddering moment when Christ said, "My God, my God, why hast thou forsaken me?" The supreme tragedy of man is to be so absorbed in this perishing world that he fails to grasp by faith what Jesus has done for him in obeying the Law and suffering the wages of sin.

The other thing which has impressed me is that, if we have surrendered ourselves to the Passion of Christ, we must speak as St. Paul does, "We thus judge that one died for all, therefore all died, and He died for all, that they that live should no longer live unto themselves, but unto Him who for their sakes died and rose again" (II Cor. 5:14 ff.). That means that Jesus Christ and covetousness cannot rule in the same heart. Either covetousness is becoming less and less or Christ is becoming less and less.

Only as we live in the invigorating atmosphere of the forgiving Word, only as we commune with the crucified and risen Christ through the Blessed Sacrament and converse with Him regularly through prayer, will covetousness grow less and Christ grow more. The musician Gounod once said, "When I was young, I used to say, 'I'; later on I said, 'I and Mozart'; then I came to the place where I said, 'Mozart and I.' But now I say, 'Mozart!'"

Christian experience parallels that. We begin with "I," our own desires—"Why was not this ointment sold?"—but as the glory of the Passion enters and fills our life, we finally come to the place where we can say, "Not I, but Christ liveth in me."

Thus the Law is fulfilled. Christ has become the beginning and the end of the Moral Law which, we previously noted, is an organic whole. Just as God is not divided, so His Law is not divided. It begins in and ends in Him who said, "I am the Alpha and the Omega."

And This Is Life Eternal

THE CONCLUSION OF THE TEN COMMANDMENTS

"I the Lord thy God am a jealous God, visiting the iniquity of the fathers upon the children unto the third
and fourth generation of them that hate Me and showing
mercy unto thousands of them that love Me and keep
My commandments."

"For Christ is the TELOS *of the law unto righteousness to everyone that believeth."*

—St. Paul

And This Is Life Eternal

"THESE WORDS SPAKE JESUS, AND LIFTED UP HIS
EYES TO HEAVEN, AND SAID, FATHER, THE HOUR
IS COME; GLORIFY THY SON, THAT THY SON ALSO
MAY GLORIFY THEE: AS THOU HAS GIVEN HIM
POWER OVER ALL FLESH, THAT HE SHOULD
GIVE ETERNAL LIFE TO AS MANY AS THOU
HAST GIVEN HIM. AND THIS IS LIFE ETERNAL,
THAT THEY MIGHT KNOW THEE THE ONLY TRUE
GOD, AND JESUS CHRIST, WHOM THOU HAST
SENT."

John 17:1-3

I N CONCLUSION I invite you to walk quietly with
me into that Upper Room where Jesus prayed His
High Priestly Prayer. The record is in John 17. We
have been there before, you and I. Not long ago we lis-
tened to the Lord of Truth pray, "Sanctify them in Thy
truth, Thy Word is truth," and we saw in that prayer
the essential meaning of the Third Commandment.

Now as we come to that portion of the Catechism
which Luther calls, "The Conclusion of the Commandments," we again listen to Jesus praying the High
Priestly Prayer. As we listen to the deliberate words and
sense the intensity of feeling in each petition, we are

aware that John 17 must surely be one of the most holy accounts in all of the Holy Scriptures.

The opening sentence of the High Priest's prayer reminds us that the earthly mission of the Priest is almost ended. The great priestly sacrifice for sin is about to be made, the climax of the atonement is at hand. The cross stands before Him. Then it is we hear the triumphant utterance: "And this is life eternal that they might know Thee, the only true God, and Jesus Christ whom Thou hast sent!"

Do you catch the passionate tone and the yearning of that ejaculatory prayer, *"And this is life eternal"*? How Christ desired to give men eternal life! How He desired the salvation of lost humanity! How He desired the cross! He knew that it was only through the cross that He could put eternal life at the disposal of humanity, according to the purpose of the Father. The prospect of joy made the cruel cross desirable. "For the joy that was set before Him He endured the cross, despising the shame."

It seems almost like trespassing for us to enter this Upper Room where Jesus is praying. We wonder, for a moment, what right we have—we with our complicated, fevered minds and sinful ways—to probe into the prayer life of Jesus which breathes such divine simplicity and confidence in the Father!

Yet, we can be sure we are not trespassing. Trespassing implies something unholy, but we are on a holy mission just now. So, "let us go with quiet mind" and learn from Jesus Christ concerning eternal life. And let us see what relationship this has to the Conclusion of the Commandments.

I

He says first that eternal life is *"To know Thee, the only true God."*

Notice what our blessed Lord says. Eternal life is not to know *about* God, but to *know* God. Let that be made clear, for there is an eternity of difference between knowing about God and knowing Him as God. The great weakness of modern men lies in just this realm. Men do not *know* God and consequently they are confused about Him, about the Church and about the world. Those who know Him are not confused, for God is "not a God of confusion" (I Cor. 14:33).

Henry Luce, publisher of *Life, Time* and *Fortune* magazines, is the son of a missionary who of late has become quite vocal in the realm of theology. Writing in the *Christian Century* (March 19, 1947), he made some statements which deserve wide circulation. I quote some of them:

"Protestantism has permitted and even encouraged . . . fuzzy ideas about God."

Here is another:

"The fashionable Protestantism of the last decade was a non-creedal, non-theological, non-ecclesiastical Protestantism. It found many passages in the Scriptures to support its intellectually fuzzy, morally weak good-willism. It relied heavily, for example, on the thirteenth chapter of First Corinthians. If Protestants know anything, they know that thirteenth chapter—'faith, hope and love, these three . . . . and the greatest of these is love.' "

I believe this indictment is true. Even in the Lutheran Church, which prides itself on its informed laity, there has been a generation of people ranging between 30 and 60 years of age who are, by and large, theologically ignorant. They grew to adulthood in an era when it was popular to scorn doctrine and creed and theology. Our untutored grandparents knew more theology than the masses of this generation. Modern man has made much of the phrases, "We have to live our Christianity," "We need practical Christianity." So he emphasized I Corinthians 13. He made love a god. To be sure God is love, but it does not follow that love is God. He spent a great deal of his time denying the authority of the Bible and then, without blushing, he turned around and quoted the Bible to support his contention that "peace on earth" comes from "good will to men."

Although Mr. Luce would be unquestionably a more effective witness for God if he changed his advertising policy, I have nevertheless quoted him at length because I too have sensed this "fuzziness" about God, this lack of clarity and exactitude, this lack of certainty. It all stems, I am confident, from the fact that men know some things *about* God but they do not *know* God. It is of this need that Christ speaks when He says, "This is life eternal that they might *know* Thee, the only true God."

One of our purposes this Lent has been to remind ourselves that it is eternally important to know *God*, not as a divine old man with a kindly face and a long gray beard, but as the real God, the Author of the Moral Law, and the Author of man's salvation. Our study of the Moral Law has helped us to know God and to understand why Luther placed the words of Exodus 20:5-6 as the Conclusion to the Commandments: "I the Lord thy God am a jealous God, visiting the iniquity of the fathers upon the children." A "jealous God" is one who will not permit sin to destroy His plan to redeem and save men. Therefore, this "jealous God" punishes sin and restrains men through the warnings of the Moral Law, and shows them their utter helplessness in being able to live so as to please Him perfectly.

Jesus, the High Priest, meant that when He said, "This is life eternal that they might know Thee, the only true God." Eternal life is to know God as a jealous God, one who insists that His law be obeyed.

II

But the glory of the Gospel is that *eternal life* is to know God as a *merciful God*. That is why our High Priest said, "This is life eternal, that they might know Thee the only true God, *and Jesus Christ, whom Thou hast sent.*" Complete knowledge of God is not possible apart from Jesus Christ who reveals the loving heart of the Father. Therefore, the purpose of the Law is not only to point us to a jealous God who visits iniquity even unto the third and fourth generation, but to show us the God who exhibits "mercy unto thousands of them that love Him and keep His commandments."

One day a good and sincere parishioner said to me, "My, it seems that everything I do is sinful. Even the good things I try to do I sense are not altogether good. And when I read God's Word, it only increases my sense of sinfulness." We turned to Romans 5 and read verses twenty and twenty-one: "Moreover, the law entered that the offense [the sense of sin] might abound. But where sin abounded, grace did much more abound; that as sin hath reigned unto death, even so might grace reign through righteousness unto eternal life by Jesus Christ our Lord." Then we turned to John's statement, "If our heart condemn us, God is greater than our heart" (I John 3:20). If there is anything that we learn from the Lenten season and its message of the Passion of Christ, it is that God is greater than our heart, that grace is stronger than sin, that God's mercy permeates His jealousy.

In spite of this, some people no doubt find a dull monotony about these forty days before Easter. To them the Lenten message is a humdrum recitation of historical data concerning the last days of Jesus of Nazareth. Thus men grow stale and fuzzy in the very shadow of the cross of Christ and hear only faintly and distortedly the High Priest's prayer, "And this is life eternal, that they may know Thee the only true God."

That is why, in the foregoing studies, I have sought to cast the traditional story of Lent in that light which, if not the only understandable one, is at least a significant and eminently needful light, namely, the Moral Law in relation to the Passion of our Lord.

CHAPTER ELEVEN

The King's Cross

Palm Sunday

"O Jesus! King most wonderful,
Thou Conqueror renowned;
Thou Sweetness most ineffable,
In whom all joys are found!"
—St. Bernard of Clairvaux

The King's Cross

"BEING FOUND IN FASHION AS A MAN, HE
HUMBLED HIMSELF, BECOMING OBEDIENT
EVEN UNTO DEATH, YEA, THE DEATH OF
THE CROSS."

Phil. 2:8

IT WAS a day something like this, soon two thousand
years ago, that Jesus entered Jerusalem. Today Jesus
enters our city. He enters every city where the Gospel is preached and the Sacraments are administered. He
comes, bringing what men need most, "the peace of God
that passeth understanding!"

There are two things which we traditionally associate
with Palm Sunday. *One is external*: the palms which
give this Sunday its name. *The other is spiritual*: a message about a King who was to die on a cross.

The palms of this festival day are like the battle flags
of our most holy faith. This is the day of the year to
hold them high. They must never be allowed to drag in
the dust and mire of defeat, no matter how our souls
may be dismayed by the terrifying power of sin and
evil. They must always stand for "Jesus, King most wonderful!" They must always be the symbols of Him who
is the Way, the Truth, and the Life. Never ought we

permit the palms to be a mere bit of church decoration on the Sunday before Easter. Rather we should exhibit them as the heralds of the monarchy of Christ, who through the cross asserts His rightful empire over all men. That, of course, is the spiritual message of Palm Sunday.

It is not too difficult for us to recreate the setting of the first Palm Sunday when our Lord entered Jerusalem riding on a lowly beast of burden, seeing the children wave their palm branches, and hearing the song of triumph: "Hosanna to the Son of David: Blessed is he that cometh in the Name of the Lord." But admittedly it is difficult to see the spiritual meaning of all this. We, like the original Palm Sunday multitude, cannot by our own reason or strength understand why the King of Heaven must die in order to become the monarch of many. Therefore, it is more than a pious gesture when we ask the Holy Spirit to guide us into the truth as we think on this Palm Sunday about "The King's Cross."

There is one section of catechetical instruction from which I derive a special enjoyment when I am teaching the confirmands. It is that portion which deals with the offices to which Christ was anointed, namely, Prophet, Priest and King. There I love to dwell. During the weeks of Lent our thoughts have been centered briefly on Christ as Priest, the One who in Himself made full sacrifice for sin. The office of a priest is to make sacrifice. He officiates at sacrifices. Jesus said, "I lay down my life of myself; no man taketh it from me!" *He* was officiating. *He* was Priest. Next Sunday we will be reminded in the Easter Gospel that our Lord entered upon His office as King when He rose triumphant over sin and death. But today on this Palm Sunday when we read of Jesus, the King, riding into Jerusalem before the consummation of the priestly sacrifice and the regal resurrection, we are nevertheless aware of *a King with a cross in the background*. It is the Priest-King who occupies the center of our thought as we enter Holy Week. It is the "King's Cross" that is the burden of the day's message.

What is there about the King's Cross that is different from other crosses? There are three marks of difference, each expressed by a single verb. The King's Cross convicts, comforts, and creates.

I

THE KING'S CROSS CONVICTS MEN

That day when Jesus was crucified between two thieves, one of the men taunted Jesus, ridiculing His claim to be Christ. The other man rebuked his one time partner in crime by saying, "Dost thou not fear God [he did!], seeing thou art in the same condemnation? And we indeed justly; for we receive the due reward of our deeds." Then indicating Christ, he said, "But this man hath done nothing amiss." In one instance the King on the cross convicted a man to judgment; in the other, he convicted to eternal life.

What a remarkable forecast of the future was that happening when the King was crucified! The world of men today responds precisely as those two robbers did. Men look at the King on the Cross and are either convicted unto judgment, or are convicted unto repentance. *In both cases they are convicted!* The cross convicts! That is why the festivities of Palm Sunday are marked by such a restrained exuberance. Your sins, my sins, the sins of our fathers, the sins of our children, the sins of the world fashioned the King's Cross. We cannot be very jubilant over that! If there had been no sin, there would have been no King's Cross.

Palm Sunday and Holy Week are God's persistent reminder that there is something terribly wrong with us. We resent being told that, but we have an uncomfortable feeling that the indictment is true. The headlines in the evening paper make us jittery, and we say, "The world is a mess!" So we turn to the comic strips for relief, bypassing the obituary column which tells an appalling story of men in their forties dying from heart disease induced by godless worry and tension. To find temporary and momentary escape from the disturbing feeling that something is wrong, men flit furtively from one excess to another. They drink intoxicants to forget. They consume aspirin by the gross. They flock to the cinema for vicarious thrills and respite from the reality of living. They drive cars at break-neck speed to premature graves. They huddle about the radio to be amused by the latest wise-cracks, and chatter stupidly in conversations about world problems when they cannot solve their own personal problems. It is a pathetic spectacle. Men and women galloping here and there in a frantic effort to escape that uncomfortable feeling that something is wrong! That feeling is intensified when men know that Christ, the King, died on a cross and said that He did so because of their sins.

For you and me today, as we look at "The King's Cross," it means that if we wish to observe Palm Sunday and Holy Week it will not be exciting as the world reckons excitement. It will mean something more than decorative palms, lovely music, hushed churches, and the good feeling that comes from being with the hundreds who throng the churches for the holy days.

The King on the Cross is the reason for our restraint. The penitent thief said, "This man hath done nothing amiss." A harsh voice from somewhere says, "Well, then who has?" Then that uncomfortable feeling comes again, for *we* know the answer. We have known it all along; but we have not wanted to admit it. You see, the King's Cross convicts!

II

THE KING'S CROSS COMFORTS

What a comfort the King on the cross must have been to that penitent thief who was being crucified with Jesus! Think of what was said: "Today thou shalt be with me in Paradise." *Here was a King with power!* Right in death's jaws, by one sweeping word He could blot out another man's whole lifetime of sin and arrears and promise him Paradise. Here was One who had power to transfer the purity of His holy life to cover the impure life of a thief. Here was One who had power to bestow the merits of His dying so that another's death might be without terror, power to cast off the specter of fear that made the prospect of eternity for the thief more painful than the festering nail wounds of a crucifixion. Because this King on the Cross had all this power, He could speak the one word that removed all fear, *"Today* thou shalt be with me in Paradise."

The thief on the cross never heard Paul preach the Gospel of justification by faith in Christ, but it is not unreasonable to assume that the peace of God which follows forgiveness was a conscious possession which this man carried in his heart those last moments of life. When he saw Jesus die, how he must have longed for the Roman soldier to come with the mallet to crush his legs, so he could run to the side of this King![1]

Thus it is that the King's Cross, at one and the same time, makes men uncomfortable and yet bestows comfort by removing guilt. It convicts and it comforts. Surely, you have sensed the conviction of the cross! Have you sensed its comfort, too? Have you sensed the exhilaration that floods the soul of a man who understands for the first time that "there is no condemnation to them that are in Christ Jesus"? If you have, then you will find no difficulty in understanding the third distinguishing mark of the King's Cross.

III

THE KING'S CROSS CREATES

God and His Word are creative. It was a creative thing that happened on Calvary. The God of Creation, who by the Word brought forth the world and all that therein

---

[1] A figure of speech suggested in *The Man of Sorrows* by Steinhaeuser

is, was actively at work creating something through the King's Cross. He was laying the foundation for II Cor. 5:17: "Therefore, if any man be in Christ, he is a new creature: old things are passed away; behold, all things are become new." So the King's Cross creates. It creates new men. It creates men in whom there is enthusiasm for Christ and His Church. It creates men who desire to serve and dare to sacrifice. *It creates men who embody the certainty of triumph.*

The man who carries in his bosom the pardon bought by the death of the Son of God carries with him an omnipotent message. He can go anywhere, and wherever he goes, he goes with confidence and a sense of being charged with a tremendous power. Because of that, he has enthusiasm for Christ and His Church's work. He is eager to be a co-worker with God. The King's Cross has given new energies, for God works through him. He can march down the highway of life with head erect, with shoulders thrust back. He knows that the palms on Palm Sunday are the battle flags of the King of Kings and the Lord of Lords who shall reign for ever and ever and of whose Kingdom there shall be no end. The King's Cross has created in him the certainty of triumph!

CHAPTER TWELVE

Thou Preparest a Table

Maundy Thursday

"*O Bread of Life from heaven,*
To weary pilgrims given,
O Manna from above:
The souls that hunger feed Thou,
The hearts that seek Thee lead Thou,
With Thy most sweet and tender love."
—ANON., LATIN, 1661

Thou Preparest a Table

"THOU PREPAREST A TABLE BEFORE ME IN
THE PRESENCE OF MINE ENEMIES."

Psalm 23:5

A T ONE time our Lord stated, "It is more blessed
to give than to receive." Sometimes, however, it
is more blessed to receive. Especially is this
true when the donor is Jesus and the recipient is a Christian believer. Can you think of any more striking example of this fact than the Holy Communion?

Let us slip back quickly in memory to that sacred
chamber, The Upper Room. It was Thursday night, the
night on which He was betrayed. Jesus and His Disciples were reclining about the Passover Table. This was
in truth the Last Supper; the Passover as an institution
had come to an end. On the table there remained the
fragments of the bread and the unused wine. From the
remnants of this ancient feast the Lamb of God now
fashioned the New Testament and the more glorious
banquet. He prepared a table and laid upon it His own
Body and Blood. Then He charged them to perpetuate
the memory of His Passion by eating and drinking unto
the remission of their sins. This table, prepared for them

117

in the presence of earthly and unearthly enemies, was henceforth to be the covenant feast of God's people.

Once Jesus had said, "It is more blessed to give." Now He showed His disciples the circumstances under which it is more blessed to receive. When He is the Host and the bidden guest says, "Thou preparest a table before me in the presence of mine enemies," then verily it is more blessed to receive.

When David first wrote this fifth verse of the Twenty-third Psalm he may have had in mind a desert fugitive, pursued by relentless enemies, finding refuge and hospitality at last in the tent of an Arab chieftain. There, while the frustrated pursuers stamped in fury at the door of the tent, the fugitive had entered that inviolable circle of desert hospitality and safety, a chieftain's tent. The unwritten law of the Arabs made it a mark of deepest depravity not to welcome the desert traveller and not to place food before him. Immediately the host became the slave of his guest. "Thou preparest a table before me in the presence of mine enemies."

Is not that what Jesus did and does for us in the Holy Communion?

I

We note first that He, the Lord Jesus, prepared this table. It is the *Lord's* Supper. Are we acutely aware of what He has prepared for us in this meal? Let us remind ourselves of it again.

He prepared divine food, the Bread of Life. It was nourishment for eternity. All the benefits of His life of sweetness and of doing good, all the benefits of His Pas-

sion and death were given to us when He said, "Take
eat; this is my body," and "Drink ye all of it; this cup is
the new testament in my blood."

Moreover, He prepared a communion; that is, a union
together with Him, with His own and for His own. We
who are to be guests are to know that He has prepared
a table where we may be one with Him and one with
one another. That which keeps men from each other
and from Him is sin. Where there is remission of sin,
there is also union with Him and with one another. The
Body of Christ was broken in order that His Body, the
Church, might remain unbroken.

> "We are not divided,
> All one body we."

He prepared a means for testifying. "As often as ye eat
this bread and drink this cup ye do show the Lord's
death till He come" (I Cor. 11:26). The essence of every
gospel sermon is the proclamation concerning the death
of Christ for human sins. Here He has prepared an opportunity for each believer to be a gospel witness. Think
of the mighty sermon which is preached by Christian
men and women as they commune! Jesus said, "Ye shall
be witnesses unto me unto the uttermost part of the
earth." There is no more powerful witness! As often as
you do this, St. Paul says, you proclaim the Lord's death
till He come. You are witnesses!

II

Secondly, we note the words "before me." Specifically,
the Lord has prepared His table for us. Dean Engstrom

of the Church of Sweden, in a little book on the Holy Communion,[1] says that Jesus prepared this table for His disciples. The disciple is then described as one who *desires to learn of Jesus,* one to whom *His Word* is dear, one who *mourns* his sins, and one who *implores* the Lord's mercy and forgiveness. As if in a summary of this, Luther says in the Small Catechism, "The words: 'For you,' require truly believing hearts."

Thus, if you are Christ's by faith, what a glorious privilege is yours! You can say, "Thou preparest a table before *me.*" It is a privilege unclouded by ambiguities. Therefore, do not hesitate to sup with Him. You *need* to; you *may;* and you are *commanded* to do so.

III

Thirdly, we are attracted by the words, "in the presence of mine enemies."

We have become accustomed to speak of the enemies of Christ and of Christians in triads. We identify the enemies this way: "The devil, the world, and our own flesh." Or we say: "Sin, Satan, and death." The one who has experienced the hunted and pursued feeling of the fugitive would perhaps declare that the latter triad is the more descriptive of our spiritual enemies.

There is the memory of sin. It was David who described the haunting, pursuing character of this enemy when He said, "My sin is ever before me." The sinner is followed by the dark and ugly procession of his transgressions.

There is the seduction of Satan. The memory of sin is

---
[1] Engstrom, *Communion Thoughts,* page 5

not the only menace to peace and quiet. There is the insidious seduction which makes inroads on the present moment. We all know that it is not a sin to be tempted, but that does not eliminate the enemy from our lives. Its approach is sometimes so stealthy that we are caught unawares; sometimes it is as obvious as a roaring lion. Sometimes temptation crouches in our very prayers or as we kneel to receive the Lord's Supper. The seduction of Satan is an agile and clever disturber of our peace—therefore, an enemy!

There is the certainty of death. This third enemy is no less relentless than the other two; yet the plain fact is that men seek to banish the thought of death into exile. Dr. Geo. Buttrick says that the average man rarely thinks of the day when his name will appear in the obituary column. If he attends a funeral, he hurries away from it with, "Too bad about Jim," and promptly tries to lose himself in something near at hand—his job, his next week's fishing trip, or his pursuit of "success." This, says Buttrick, should be called, "the twentieth century evasion."[1] Sometimes it is good medicine to contemplate the rider on the pale horse, of whom the Book of Revelation says, "His name . . . . was Death." Death is no friend! It is an enemy! The last enemy!

It is a significant conclusion, is it not, that there is a table "in the presence of mine enemies"? Enemies that are pledged to do me harm, enemies that conspire together to destroy me! Can you not see them, drawing a hostile ring about me, chafing to rush upon my be-

---

[1] Buttrick, *Christ and Man's Dilemma,* page 24

leaguered soul? With the psalmist I would cry, "Oh, that I had wings like a dove; for then would I fly away and be at rest." Then I am reassured by those grand words, "Thou preparest a table before me *in the presence of mine enemies.*"

Christ is the fugitive's refuge! In Him we are free from the memory of sin; in Him we are strong to overcome the seduction of Satan; in Him we are valiant in the face of death. There is something exuberantly triumphant and splendidly defiant about the man who can cry out, "'Thou preparest a table before me in the presence of mine enemies."

Come, let us sup with Him and with one another at the Table of the Lord.

CHAPTER THIRTEEN

That Monument
of Victory

Good Friday

"What language shall I borrow
    To thank Thee, dearest Friend,
For this Thy dying sorrow,
    Thy pity without end?
Oh, make me Thine forever;
    And should I fainting be,
Lord, let me never, never,
    Outlive my love to Thee."
        —ST. BERNARD OF CLAIRVAUX

That Monument of Victory

"CHRIST HAVING COME A HIGH PRIEST OF
THE GOOD THINGS TO COME, THROUGH THE
GREATER AND MORE PERFECT TABER-
NACLE, NOT MADE WITH HANDS . . . NOR
YET THROUGH THE BLOOD OF GOATS AND
CALVES, BUT THROUGH HIS OWN BLOOD,
ENTERED IN ONCE FOR ALL INTO THE
HOLY PLACE, HAVING OBTAINED ETERNAL
REDEMPTION."

Hebrews 9:11-12

TO SOME it may seem like an affectation to describe the cross as "That Monument of Victory." Yet, if what we have described during these days of Lent be true, Good Friday in its deepest meaning is a day not of tragedy but of triumph. For the Christian, Good Friday and Easter are closely united. The one cannot be understood without the other. It is not strange, therefore, that Luther did not write a single Passion hymn. His Easter hymns, however, contemplate both the Suffering Savior and the Risen Lord. One of them, "Christ Jesus lay in death's strong bands,"[1] has this striking stanza:

[1] See *The Lutheran Hymnary*, No. 330

125

> "It was a strange and dreadful strife
>   When Life and death contended;
> The victory remained with Life,
>   The reign of death was ended;
> Stripped of power, no more he reigns;
> An empty form alone remains;
>   His sting is lost for ever!"

What graphic words Luther uses to picture what transpired when our High Priest entered into the Holy of Holies to obtain for us "eternal redemption"! "Dreadful strife," "Life and death contended," "death . . . stripped of power"—all this took place when Christ went beyond the veil to make sacrifice once for all for the sins of His brethren.

Sometimes I have wondered how far we are permitted to probe into the mystery of the cross. How did Christ's death defeat sin and death? How could He who is "very God of very God" be forsaken by God? How could He be both Priest and Sacrifice? Certainly there was something hidden, inscrutable, and unutterable about that first Good Friday. And yet the question persists: How far may we venture into this holy mystery?

I suggest that the answer lies in our text and the Old Testament type of which it is the fulfillment. We should recall on this Good Friday the Levitical account of the annual Day of Atonement for Israel. On that great day the high priest made sacrifice for the congregation and for himself. When the climactic portion of the ceremony was to take place, the congregation was not permitted to witness the sacred event. The high priest disappeared

behind the veil into the Holy of Holies. There, hidden
from human eyes and in the presence of God alone, the
atonement was wrought. But when he emerged, the congregation knew that their forgiveness had been assured!

Thus it is with the cross of Christ. When Jesus died
our death at Calvary, He, our High Priest, entered the
Holy of Holies. God has not permitted us to follow
Him there and to see all that happened during that
sacrifice. We have not been permitted to accompany
Jesus behind the veil into the Holy of Holies. What
transpired in that invisible world we shall perhaps
never know. In fact, I dare say we would rather never
know. The awfulness of the full impact of sin, death,
and hell upon the Sinless One is something, thank God,
we need not know. The immensity of human guilt, the
unmitigated, undiminished wrath of God, the madden-
ing, terrifying curse of the Law, the eternity of death—
all this was suffered by our High Priest who said of His
life, "No one taketh it away from me, but I lay it down
of myself. I have power to lay it down, and I have
power to take it again."

Although the mighty battle against the "principali-
ties and powers" and the presentation of the sacrifice
to God was hidden from prying eyes, we, nevertheless,
have some intimations of that "strange and dreadful
strife, when Life and death contended." Already in
Gethsemane the agony of the Lord was revealed when
He sweat great drops of blood. Moreover we can sense
the fierceness of that struggle against sin and death
as He hung upon the cross. Issuing forth from the

cavernous depths of that realm where the conflict with those tyrants raged was the piercing and anguished cry, "My God, my God, why hast thou forsaken me?" Still unable to look beyond the veil into that Holy of Holies, we nevertheless may hear, if we listen intently, that sigh of relief and gasp of victory, "It is finished!" Then we know that sin and death lie limp and defeated. Then we know that Christ the Priest has become Christ the King.

Thus, like the congregation of ancient Israel, when we see our High Priest emerge from the Holy of Holies, we are assured that our redemption has been won, and Easter's empty tomb will testify to us that the cruel cross is now transfigured with an eternal glow. Indeed, it has become what St. Athanasius called it, "That Monument of Victory."

> "So let us keep the festival
>   Whereto the Lord invites us;
>   Christ is Himself the joy of all,
>   The Sun that warms and lights us;
>   By His grace He doth impart
>   Eternal sunshine to the heart;
>   The night of sin is ended!"
>   —M. LUTHER, 1524

CHAPTER FOURTEEN

Easter Power for This Hour

Easter Day

"Lord, by the stripes which wounded Thee,
From death's dread sting Thy servants free,
That we may live and sing to Thee,
Hallelujah!"

ANON., LATIN, 1753

Easter Power for This Hour

"THAT I MAY . . . BE FOUND IN HIM, NOT HAVING
MINE OWN RIGHTEOUSNESS, WHICH IS OF THE
LAW, BUT THAT WHICH IS THROUGH THE
FAITH OF CHRIST . . . THAT I MAY KNOW HIM,
AND THE POWER OF HIS RESURRECTION."

Phil. 3:9-10

I ASK you this Easter to think about a sublime subject, *"Easter Power for This Hour."* Very quickly let me describe "this hour" in which we live.

This is an hour of uncertainty. Men are bewildered, frustrated, and discouraged. All over the world the story is the same. The common people are hungry and tired. The cause? War and its shambles. Edward Benes of Czechoslovakia said of the people of Europe following the first World War, "We are so weary!" What must he be saying after World War II when men are feverishly preparing for World War III? Yes, this is an hour of *uncertainty.*

This is an hour of apprehension. Apprehension is closely related to uncertainty. It means fear. Fear, like a lethal fog, has been creeping over the minds and spirits of men. Lurking behind many of our fears is the atom bomb, which we fear somebody may steal from us and use against us. Dr. L. W. Boe, the late president of St. Olaf College, used to say, "When the fear of God leaves a people, the fear of man sets in."

This is an hour of moral decay. A man's word seems to mean little any more. A contract is no longer a morally binding instrument, whether it is a marriage contract, or a contract between management and labor. The mad pursuit of godless pleasure only sharpens the focus in this tragic picture of moral decay. The wrecked lives and broken homes, the staggering sums of wasted money, and the mounting number of neurotic cases are stark reminders of disintegration. This is an hour of moral decay.

This hour is an hour of urgency. The organized Church is in danger from enemies without and within. In Europe the Church is in danger of extinction from godless philosophies, militant Communism and latent Fascism. In the Orient it is threatened by the very weight and immensity of the heathen world without the Gospel. At home in America it is confronted by a militant, powerful, wealthy, intelligent pagan force. In a state like Minnesota where seventy percent of the people were in favor of the governor's program of civic righteousness, a powerful moneyed minority was almost successful in attempts to kill a program to bring decency into public life. All these are enemies outside the Church. The greatest cause for anxiety, however, is the enemy within the Church. The Church is not well. It is sick because there are many who claim to be followers of Christ but who are not even reasonable facsimiles of the same. They are not even clever hypocrites! They are weak in faith, uncertain about their own salvation, flabby and loose in their morals, and stingy in their giving. They have never heard, or have forgotten, what Jesus said, "He that is not with me, is against me" (Matt. 12:30).

This hour, therefore, is an hour of *uncertainty, apprehension, moral decay,* and, because of all this, an hour of *urgency.* I have deliberately painted this picture with bold, dark strokes. This is no hysterical, unreasoned outburst. It is studied and purposeful. It is a deadly earnest attempt to present the hopelessness of men without God, so that the Gospel of Easter will be radiant in this hour of gloom.

The grand message of the open tomb is that there is "Easter Power for This Hour." The tragedy of our Easters is that that power is not comprehended nor is it utilized. To that end, that is, to the comprehension and utilization of that power, we must, under God, dedicate this Easter, not next Easter. That may be too late! There may not be many more opportunities in these apocalyptic days to tell men that there is "Easter Power for This Hour."

How can we do that? Let me suggest that we must be sure of three things.

I

Easter power is based on an event in history. It is historic reality. Of that we must be sure! The task which we have set before us today does not permit us to dwell very long on the historic fact of the resurrection. But since it is so fundamental to what follows we must pause a moment.

The Christian Gospel means little without the certainty that Jesus Christ is risen from the dead. "It is well to remember that no item of our Christian faith can be scientifically demonstrated. There is a sense in which we must ever walk by faith and not by sight. . . . Yet it is also well to remember that faith rests on evidence, and that this evidence is sufficient for faith. That is true of the resurrection of Jesus Christ" (J. P. Milton).

One of the most remarkable things about the resurrection in the New Testament record, which is thereby a testimony to the reality of the resurrection, is the emphasis on the *doubts* of Jesus' disciples.[1] They were in a dubious and skeptical frame of mind and were "not ready to accept hearsay testimony." Had the story of the resurrection been a fabrication, the perpetrators of this fantastic narrative would in all likelihood have emphasized the *faith* of the disciples instead of their doubts. But we are even told in the narrative that one apostle, Thomas, kept his doubts for a whole week before he was convinced.

The faith of the early Christians in the actual bodily resurrection of Jesus, therefore, was not gullibility, but an open-eyed belief "built on accumulative and irresistible evidence," such as Luke records in the Book of Acts (1:3) : "He showed Himself alive after His passion by many infallible proofs, being seen of them forty days."

---

[1] Zwemer, *The Glory of the Cross*, page 120

And Paul tells us (I Cor. 15) that over five hundred Christians saw and recognized Jesus.

Easter power is based on an event in history. That is the first thing of which we must be sure.

II

The second conviction we must entertain is that Easter power is regnant through the person and work of Christ who is alive forevermore.

There is danger in stressing the historical fact of the resurrection. It is here that we are prone to dwell. This we must not do if we would know "the power of the resurrection." We begin with the historic fact, but we must not remain there.

Sometimes we have made of Easter a memorial day, and of our Easter services, memorial services. We memorialize a fact in history which seems to exert little power in the present, except as other memorial days exert their benign influence. Sometimes when I come to the end of Easter Day, I am smitten with the awful thought that thousands of people who have attended Easter services have "taken the name of the Lord in vain" by merely commemorating the fact that Christ rose from the grave and said, "because I live ye shall live also." Then they go home and say, "My, wasn't there a big crowd in church and wasn't Mary's new hat pretty!"

If we would know the meaning of Easter power, we must know that it rules only through the person and work of Jesus Christ, who is alive now and forevermore. That I believe is the explanation of St. Paul's passionate expression in our text today: "That I might know Him and the power of His resurrection!" Notice how he unites resurrection power with the knowledge of Christ, not with a fact of history, but with a living Person! "Easter power" is merely a religious phrase to a man unless he first *knows* Christ and is "found in Him." The glorious doctrine of justification by faith is this! To be "found in Him" means to hide our sinful selves in the Rock of Ages cleft for us on the Good Friday cross.

If this talk about Easter power is all quite incomprehensible to you, it is doubtless due to one thing: *you do not know Christ as the Living One and you are not "found in Him."*

That is why it is so futile to preach the resurrection and Easter power to unsaved people. Paul had that experience. He came once to Athens in Greece, the center of great learning and philosophy. He had been invited to preach by certain "philosophers" who were curious to hear this new teaching about Jesus of Nazareth. In his sermon on Mars Hill (Acts 17), Paul strongly emphasized the resurrection of Jesus. But when he got to that point, *he lost his audience.* The record tells us that most of his hearers mocked him and sneered at the idea of the resurrection. A few, out of courtesy, expressed a willingness to listen to him again. But Paul was a beaten man. He left the city and went to Corinth conscious of his dismal failure to take advantage of a distinguished occasion to preach the Gospel. Some time later Paul wrote a letter to the congregation he organized at Corinth. As if still smarting under his failure when he had preached the resurrection at Athens, he confesses to the Corinthians that he had come to Corinth, "determined to know nothing among them save Jesus Christ and *Him crucified.*"[1]

That is what I mean when I say that if we would know Easter power for this hour, we must know it as being present only in the person and work of Jesus. It is regnant through Him who not only suffered death because of our sins, but who *conquered death* by the power of God. Thus we would point out that not only does the Moral Law help us to understand the Passion of Christ, but it makes more comprehensible the resurrection of Christ.

III

The third thing of which we must be sure is that resurrection power is available right now and is to be utilized right now! It is "Easter power for *this* hour!"

What is this power? It is not some spiritually explosive power that if used will suddenly make the world well by bringing peace to distraught nations. It is not something which if introduced at the Four Power Conference in Moscow[2] would make everybody congenial and happy and easy to get along with. Nor is Easter power something to be compared to or even matched against atomic power. *To do any of these is to prostitute the message of Easter and to make it something less than it is!* Easter is with us to set in bold relief the hopelessness of a world

---

[1]"The Transfigured Cross," *The Christian Century*, March 29, 1944.
[2]Representatives of the Four Powers were meeting during Easter, 1947, at Moscow.

without Christ. It is to magnify, not to minimize, the gloom and despair, the bitterness and hunger, the hate and strife, the immorality and shame of men without Christ. It is to make us aware that this is the undying characteristic of a "world that lieth in the power of the evil one" (I John 5:19), the optimistic and idealistic preachers of social righteousness to the contrary notwithstanding! And all this stark, unrelieved Easter emphasis on gloom is so that we will not be tempted to make of Easter power something less than it really is. It is not some divine medicine to make this sick world well, to doctor it up and make it more livable and pleasant. That can be and ought to be a by-product of Easter power, but it is not the end and goal of the resurrection.

Easter power for this hour is the risen Christ dwelling in believers, enabling them to live their lives *above* the sin and death of earth, not in mystic seclusion and withdrawal from the world, but in the midst of the world where they can be the salt of the earth! It is the life of Christian faith which Jesus proclaimed at the grave of Lazarus: "I am the resurrection and the life; he that *believeth* in me .... shall never die." Or as Paul says in Romans 6: *"Know ye not that so many of us as were baptized into Jesus Christ were baptized into his death? Therefore, we are buried with him by baptism into death: that like as Christ was raised up from the dead by the glory of the Father, even so we also should walk in newness of life. For if we have been planted together in the likeness of his death, we shall be also in the likeness of his resurrection. .... Likewise, reckon ye yourselves to be dead unto sin, but alive unto God through Jesus Christ our Lord."*

That is the real essence of Easter power, to be "alive unto God," to live "the risen life" with Christ!

Practically speaking, this Easter power is demonstrated in only two ways:

First, in our new found power over sin. That means also power over death, for where there is power over sin there is power over death. "The sting of death is sin." Some Christians do not utilize this Easter power, I fear. They live feebly because they coddle some pet sin. They have surrendered themselves to Christ, but some areas of their lives are still under the dominion of sin. Here is a Christian woman who loves to gossip. Or here is a man who has not put his income at the disposal of God. Or there is a person with a violent temper. All of these are Christian, and men say, "How can that be?" Let us remember that when the Japanese surrendered to Mac-Arthur, there were still some outlying garrisons of soldiers who refused to surrender. These were the die-hards. Thus we too may surrender to Christ while some areas of our life are still dominated by sin. Consequently there is mopping up work to do. Easter power for this hour means that every area of our life into which Christ is permitted entrance is *conquered for Him.* That is how we become "more than conquerors" through Him who loved us!

The second demonstration of Easter power is in our new-found ability to do God's will.

What is God's will? Reduced to its essentials it is found

in I Tim. 2:4: God wills that all men "be saved and come to the knowledge of the truth." Everything else in the will of God is subordinate and ancillary to the salvation of the human race. If this is God's will, and if it is true that in Christ's bestowal of the forgiveness of sins He supplies the power to perform it, then it becomes imperative that we begin right here and now to utilize the Easter power which is intended for this hour. He has made this power available in Christ for the doing of His will: evangelism, missions, the building of new churches, anything that is directed to the salvation of men. That is "Easter Power for This Hour." There is no power on earth to compare with it, for it is the Gospel, the power of God unto salvation.

Come, let us go joyfully to our task, for "night cometh"—oh, so quickly!

DATE DUE

DEMCO 38-297